THE BIG MOVIE

A GUIDE TO STANLEY KUBRICK'S
BARRY LYNDON

JOHN STRELOW

First published in 2023

Copyright John Strelow, 2023

ISBN: 9781093167252

Imprint: Independently published

Still from *Barry Lyndon* on page 16 copyright Warner Bros. and used for educational purposes only

Still from *Hell's Angels* on page 17 public domain

TABLE OF CONTENTS

PREFACE
THE BIG MOVIE

BARRY LYNDON WAS SPOKEN OF in hushed tones in the household of my childhood. Long before I was old enough to watch or appreciate it, I had been conditioned to admire the famous candle-lit photography and the strict classical music score. It was always something beyond, to be aspired to; it was The Big Movie.

There is a brief exposure of four nipples in the film, and as good and attentive parents, mine forbade me from watching lest such adult sights be revealed to me at too young an age. (Even more off-limits was another film my father spoke of in lofty terms: *A Clockwork Orange.*) It was my enrollment in a European History course in the tenth grade that finally created the excuse my father needed to persuade my mother of the necessity of my being added to the film's relatively scant audience.

I was arrested from the first combination of sound and image: the old, brief, bubbly "W" of the mid-1970s Saul Bass Warner Bros. logo creeping out of the screen to fill the eyes, accompanied by the assault of Leonard Rosenman's Oscar-winning arrangement of a Handel sarabande to fill the ears. Three hours later I was prepared to state that *Barry Lyndon* was the best movie I had ever seen.

This was some years ago, and though I went through some period of wavering (where for some stretches of time I might prefer the aforementioned and afore-banned *A Clockwork Orange*), I hold the same opinion today. It is an opinion I've never fully understood, nor have I fully understood my (now late) father's devotion to this film as well as the balance of the Kubrick oeuvre. For what could a farmer's son from Nebraska have in common with a lawyer's son from Ireland – or a doctor's son from New York?

Quite a bit, at least in the latter case. Both born in 1928, coming of age in an America ravaged by Depression and World War. Neither having the opportunity to attend college, both autodidacts who read incessantly and about deep topics (my father preferring theology, Kubrick secular philosophy, fiction, and nonfiction). Both with a keen interest in Germany and Germanic traditions, my father by way of his ethnic heritage (his father had come from the old country in the late nineteenth century) and Kubrick, apparently, by his fascination with the clash between Germany's historic aesthetic prowess and the considerable evil its people had wreaked upon Kubrick's own ethnic compatriots while under Hitler's sway. Both men had an apparently-related devotion to classical music.

Yet, there were differences: the rurally-raised Lutheran who stayed a believer his whole life vs. the urban secular Jew who declared allegiance to no earthly religion (still, he devoted more of his artistic efforts to considerations of eternity and fate than any other American film artist of his age). My father was the youngest child of a large family, Kubrick the eldest of a mere two children. My father started in the plains of the midwest and moved west, settling in the urban/suburban sprawl of Los Angeles; Kubrick fled the metropolis of New York and went east, back across the pond, foregoing Hollywood life and living in the isolated countryside. My father was a working man, familiar with hotels and restaurants and sales; Kubrick, of course, gained a (sometimes unfair) reputation as a man living a life of relative physical isolation.

Kubrick found a way to bridge what gaps there were, between himself and my father, and between himself and so many others who feel such deep kinship to his films. Despite a reputation for cold precision assigned to Kubrick by his detractors (and even some of his supporters), those of us who subscribe to Kubrickian ways find his works endlessly fascinating, intellectually provocative, and genuinely moving. And each of us has his own flagship upon which to set sail. For me, as for my father before me, I fly the colors of The Big Movie.

CHAPTER ONE
THE LUCK OF STANLEY KUBRICK

BARRY LYNDON WAS NOT the first historical epic either completed or contemplated by Stanley Kubrick. As for the former, his *Spartacus* is more important for Kubrick biographically than artistically, as his unsatisfactory work-for-hire experience drove him from that point forward to secure and exercise strict control of his films from conception through release. Of more relevance was his failure, in the years immediately following the release and success of *2001: A Space Odyssey*, to make a feature film of the life of Napoleon.

Kubrick's *Napoleon* is one of the most famous of unmade films, and earned its status as such owing to commercial anxiety on the behalf of potential financiers, brought about by both the high budget Kubrick's conception would have incurred and the then-recent box office failure of Sergey Bondarchuk's *Waterloo*, which starred Rod Steiger as the Corsican conqueror. It is clear from *Barry Lyndon's* existence that Kubrick's desire to depict an epic tale of continental Europe was not quenched by this experience, and it is clear from his comments on the unmade project that several of the themes that appealed to him in a telling of Napoleon's life were also extant in the Thackeray novel that he did manage to bring to the screen.

Kubrick's drive to tell a story that encompassed all elements of an age date back to at least the early 1960s, when in an essay he wrote for *The Observer Weekend Review* he stated that he "would like to make a film that gave a feeling of the times -- a contemporary story that finally gave a feeling of the times, psychologically, sexually, politically, personally" (Kubrick OWR). Modify the "contemporary" setting qualifier, and the remaining attributes resonate with Kubrick's response to interviewer Joseph Gelmis' 1970 query as to what attracted him to the life of Bonaparte: "I find," Kubrick said, "that all the issues with which [the story of Napoleon's life] concerns itself are oddly contemporary – the responsibilities and abuses of power, the dynamics of social revolution, the relationship of the individual to the state, war, militarism, etc. ... [*Napoleon* will be] a film about the basic questions *of our own times*" (emphasis mine) (Gelmis 297). Like the auteurs of Hollywood before him, it appears that Kubrick found it more expedient to explore a panoply of contemporary issues by addressing them indirectly, finding historical analogues for modern dilemmas; as he told Gelmis, "the basic purpose of a film, which I believe is one of illumination [...] showing the viewer something he can't see any other way. And I think at times this can be best accomplished by staying away from dealing with his own immediate environment" (300).

Though Kubrick's interest in grand political issues comes as no surprise from the director of *Dr. Strangelove, A Clockwork Orange*, and *Full Metal Jacket*, one cannot overlook the attraction Napoleon's personal life had to Kubrick the dramatist. Continuing his answer to Gelmis explaining the intrigue of Napoleon, Kubrick pointed out that beyond "those [political and philosophical] aspects of the story, the sheer drama and force of Napoleon's life is a fantastic subject for a film biography. Forgetting everything else and just taking Napoleon's romantic involvement with Josephine, for example, here you have one of the great obsessional passions of all time (297). ("His sex life was worthy of Arthur Schnitzler," he added [ibid.], years before his desire to adapt *Traumnovelle* was known or achieved.)

Kubrick's screenplay for *Napoleon*, which was available for years online before being officially released in the Alison Castle-edited *Stanley Kubrick's "Napoleon": The Greatest Movie Never Made*, devotes considerable focus to Napoleon's personal life. Kubrick's interviews with Napoleon biographer Felix Markham, published in the same volume and annotated by Geoffrey Ellis, interrogate not only the social and political context of Napoleon's career, but his motivating psychology. Markham described Napoleon's background to Kubrick as being similar to Scottish highlanders, a people "rather barbaric as compared with Parisians, but definitely noble, not bourgeois, like poorish Highland squires" (Ellis 94). This paints a picture of an outsider, a position Napoleon also, as Kubrick and Markham discussed, found himself in relative to other monarchs. "[H]e wasn't one of them," Markham pronounced (112). Napoleon went out of his way to remind the other kings "that they were kings by blood and he was king by achievement. ... He was just not one of them." "Obviously," Kubrick responded, "he must have felt that in a thousand ways when he was dealing with them. ... You know, in every conceivable way people communicate things psychologically and emotionally. He must have felt this all the time" (ibid.).

Kubrick was deeply interested in this outsider dynamic, and in dramatizing it in his film. "I think it's very, very important in the scenes – it'll have to be done subtly – but it's very important, I think, to portray in this very subtle way their attitude about him, the way they feel about him, and the way they treat him, and what they think about him," he told Markham (113). "I mean, he wouldn't have had such a bad time of it if they weren't so offended by him."

It is easy to see why the storyteller in Kubrick would be so keen to identify the psychological motivations of both Napoleon and his foils. But one wonders why it was specifically Napoleon that attracted Kubrick above all other similar figures, from times ancient to modern. Kubrick was, in the public sphere, guarded about his own personal feelings, but perhaps we can find some fruit by luxuriating in informed speculation. Could Kubrick have seen some of himself in the French Emperor? On a superficial level, one might draw a parallel between the logistical genius required of Napoleon to mount his military campaigns and the organizational regimen Kubrick imposed upon all of his post-*Spartacus* productions. But this parallel would reside in the biography of any great military commander. It might seem that one aspect of Napoleon's personality and career that appealed to Kubrick was Napoleon's status as self-made man, as a genius who worked his way from outside the concentrated circles of privilege into them by merit and drive. Kubrick did not rise to the top of his profession (and even his detractors must admit that his professional status, under which Warner Bros. funded his films with a combination of Medici-esque level of dedication and *laissez faire* management, is singular and enviable in the history of the American film industry) from within it, moving up a ladder from apprentice to the top, but by making his own way, shooting short documentaries and securing funding for features outside of the Hollywood studio system, a system to which he never truly belonged even at the many peaks of his career.

With outsider status comes fear and paranoia, sometimes justified, and here we may step into even muddier waters as we consider, as has been the fashion in critical circles in the years since Kubrick's passing, the effect that Kubrick's Jewish background had on his life and work. Frederic Raphael, in his account of adapting Schnitzler's *Traumnovelle* into *Eyes Wide Shut*, opened this can of worms in his descriptions of Kubrick speaking of his background, which caused some headline writers to assert that Raphael was describing Kubrick as a "self-hating Jew" (a phrase that does not actually appear in Raphael's pages). Raphael does present an image of Kubrick cloistered within a non-Gentile world and paranoid (Raphael does use that word) about it; discussing a potential *Eyes Wide Shut* scene wherein two men are seen talking, Kubrick pressed Raphael on the details of their conversation:

[Kubrick]:	Couple of Gentiles, right?
[Raphael]:	That's what you wanted them to be.
SK:	Coupla Jews, what do we know about what those people talk about when they're by themselves?
FR:	Stanley, come *on*, those people! You've heard

6

> them talking. They talk about much the same
> kind of things we talk about, *don't they*? I
> mean, you've heard them, haven't you, at the
> next table in restaurants, in front of you in
> theaters and, ah, places? I have and ...
>
> SK: Maybe, but I'll tell you something: they always
> know you're there (Raphael 105-106).

"He wasn't one of them," said Markham of Napoleon. Kubrick: "He must have felt this all the time." We are, perhaps, on less than solid ground here, for Raphael's account of working with Kubrick has been disputed in both fact and spirit by those on friendly (or familial) terms with the director, and in fact one might observe that Raphael's work, subtitled *A Memoir of Stanley Kubrick*, might have been more accurately subtitled *An Agonistes of Frederic Raphael*. Michael Herr, another writing collaborator of Kubrick's (*Full Metal Jacket*), also discussed the fact of Kubrick's Jewishness is his far more generous reminiscence of Kubrick in *Vanity Fair*, which was later published as its own monograph. Herr recounts Kubrick keeping him informed of news items of anti-Semitism (or its decline), and also reports that Kubrick urged him to read Raul Hilberg's "enormous" history of the Holocaust, *The Destruction of the European Jews* (Herr).

We know that the Holocaust fascinated Kubrick as a dramatic subject, and he long pursued adapting Louis Begley's Holocaust-set novel *Wartime Lies* into a film that would have been titled *Aryan Papers*. He also explored the possibility of making a film about the jazz scene under Nazi rule (Frewin 517) (his admiration of Bob Fosse's *Cabaret*, which led to Marisa Berenson's casting in *Lyndon*, may reflect his interest in this subject and period, as well). It is neither strange nor surprising that a man born into a Jewish family (even a secular one) in 1928 would take a keen interest in a genocide aimed at his people, and while Kubrick never dramatized the Holocaust directly, some have argued (most notably Geoffrey Cocks in *The Wolf at the Door: Stanley Kubrick, History, and the Holocaust*, and more publicly proclaimed by Cocks' appearance in the documentary on fan theories regarding *The Shining*, *Room 237*) that his interest in it and attitudes toward it seep through into his oeuvre (and even that, somewhat counterintuitively, this interest found its greatest flowering in *The Shining*).

Litigating such questions is outside of our purview here, but sufficient evidence exists to suggest that Kubrick did feel that his Jewish background was intrinsic to his identity and, if Raphael is to be believed, how he saw himself interacting with the world at large (it is notable that a world-touring exhibition of artifacts from Kubrick's archives made its San Francisco landing at The Contemporary Jewish Museum). It is inviting to assign aspects of a "Jewish identity" to Kubrick and subsequently his work, and one might jump to making parallels between a people that for so long lived in exile from their homeland and a director who was an expatriate, a dictator who twice found himself exiled from his one-time empire, and a young Irishman living a "wandering existence" making his fortune on the continent and in Britain, only to find no trust or friendships among his betters and himself banished from the palatial estates he had so dearly pursued and the adopted homeland he had tried to make his own.

And while it is foolhardy to psychoanalyze any stranger, and much moreso a figure as private as Kubrick was, I daresay we are not out of line in assuming that Kubrick took pride in his independence and the work he put in to secure it, given the importance it held in his life and career. Again, we see such pride in outsidership in the Napoleonic psychology that Kubrick discussed with Felix Markham; we also see it in the rise and fall of Redmond Barry.

Kubrick told Michel Ciment, in response to a question as to what led him to adapt *Barry Lyndon*, "I can't honestly say what led me to make any of my films. The best I can do is say I just fell in love with the stories. Going beyond that is a bit like trying to explain why you fell in love with your wife: she's intelligent, has brown eyes, a good figure. Have you really said anything?" (Ciment 167) Kubrick was notoriously close to the vest, at least so far as his interactions with interlocutors and collaborators were concerned (both writers and actors have reported that he could be minimal with direction [e.g., telling Malcolm McDowell "Malcolm, I'm not RADA [the Royal Academy of Dramatic Art]. I hired *you* to do the acting" {Herr}], often discovering what he wanted from a script or performance by being shown [and thus eliminating] what he did not), but it would uncharitable and unproductive of us to not take him at his word. Still, in examining Kubrick's mature works, it is not difficult to find resonances between his biography and the themes and situations of his productions. Kubrick's detractors frequently portray him as a cold, overly logical filmmaker who is more concerned with ideas (and cinematographic technology) than people, but his is a cinema as personal as any we have seen.

Dr. Strangelove: or, How I Learned to Stop Worrying and Love the Bomb is as good a starting point as any, as it was the first of his mature films he produced without a partner. One unmistakable, but little-discussed, element of the film is that in his portrayal of President Merkin Muffley, Peter Sellers' accent is very similar to Kubrick's. It may be that

Kubrick's Bronx lilt was merely utilized by Sellers as it was one of the few American voices on the British set, but Muffley's constant ping-ponging of questions off of his advisors mirrors the critic Alexander Walker's statement about the director that:

> [h]is conversation was endlessly interrogative. This was sometimes abrupt or disconcerting when rapid-fire questions pushed one up against the wall of one's own inability to come out with satisfying answers. [...] Communicating with Kubrick was a kind of "debriefing" – the military term is quite appropriate – for his need to inform himself fully before he made decisions was obsessive (Walker 8-9).

Kubrick's fastidiousness and dedication to organization and plans is legendary (a documentary, *Stanley Kubrick's Boxes*, has even been made regarding his penchant for organization). It is thus striking that so many of Kubrick's narratives focus on the disintegration of well-made plans; it is almost as though Kubrick was exploring the limitations of his own approach to life through his films, and the intricate plans, based in logic and upended by fallibility and inopportune emotion, come apart as an embodiment of his nightmares. His most explicitly nightmarish film is, of course, *The Shining*, the story of a creative man living remotely from society who loses his grip once he is cut off from the world. Kubrick's monastical lifestyle has been well-documented, but equally documented was his penchant for telephonic conversation ("I've been hearing about all the people who say they talked to Stanley on the last day of his life, and however many of them there were, I believe them all," wrote Michael Herr [Herr]); being cut off from that world, and being alienated from his family, might well have been one of Kubrick's deepest fears. "Failure of communication is a theme that runs through a number of my films," Kubrick admitted to Ciment (Ciment 188).

One can point to other superficial linkages between Kubrick and his characters: foolproof systems of logic go awry in *The Killing*, *Dr. Strangelove*, *2001: A Space Odyssey*, and even the ill-fated Ludovico Treatment in *A Clockwork Orange*; Kubrick's career start as a photojournalist for *Look* magazine corresponds to the *Stars & Stripes* staff manned by Matthew Modine's Joker and Kevyn Major's Rafterman (Rafterman, like Kubrick before him, is a photographer, and his "arc" from combat naïve to hardened killer reminds one of John Milius quoting Kubrick as saying "I feel perfectly safe in my love of war and military history because I know that I'm a devout coward" [Bogdanovich]) in *Full Metal Jacket*; and *Eyes Wide Shut* is a film made by a New York doctor's son who married a painter about a New York doctor who married an art gallery owner. It would be mistaken to try to reduce Kubrick's films or his choices of stories to adapt to these glancing similarities, but it seems possible, if not likely, that such factors may have influenced Kubrick in his story choices, regardless of any conscious awareness of such an effect on his part.

There are other apparent influences on *Barry Lyndon*, and two cinematic precedents come to mind: *Gone with the Wind* will be briefly examined in Chapter 8, but Kubrick thought highly of *The Godfather*. Herr describes Kubrick "reluctantly suggesting for the 10th time that it was possibly the greatest movie ever made, and certainly the best-cast" (Herr), and Vincent LoBrutto's essential biography of Kubrick quotes *Lyndon's* music arranger Leonard Rosenman as making the incredible claim that Kubrick had asked him to make a period-appropriate arrangement of Nino Rota's theme from Coppola's film (LoBrutto 404). (Accounts compiled from Kubrick's archives show the director actually sought to retain Rota to arrange the music for the film; not wanting to serve as an arranger in lieu of composing his own themes, Rota politely declined the invitation [Gengaro 149-150].) *The Godfather* was a commercially popular work that drew critical attention not only for its fine craftwork, but as a story of America in microcosm; Coppola weaved under a pulp veneer a personal story of family with a depiction of an America disillusioned of its ideals. It was, perhaps, a "(nearly) contemporary story that finally gave a feeling of the times, psychologically, sexually, politically, personally." It was exactly the kind of film Kubrick had long sought to make, and he found his own opportunity to meld personal concerns with global ones in his adaptation of a William Makepeace Thackeray novel that began its life as the serial *The Luck of Barry Lyndon*.

CHAPTER TWO
KUBRICK'S GRANDEST GAMBLE

JOSEPH GELMIS' 1970 COMPILATION of director interviews, cited previously, was entitled *The Film Director as Superstar.* His interview of Kubrick was the closing interview of the book, and it is certainly arguable that Kubrick was the director most deserving of the "superstar" appellation at the time. *Spartacus* had been a critical and box office success, *Lolita* a cause célèbre, and *Dr. Strangelove* and *2001* a one-two punch that bought him counterculture cred and critical attention. The release of *A Clockwork Orange* in December of 1971 only furthered Kubrick's notoriety in all quarters; the film was debated on editorial pages both for its content and for its mere existence, as the suitability of its violent images was a touching point for age-old debates about the behavioral effects of violent and sexual art on its audiences.

Despite being unable to bring *Napoleon* to the screen, the Stanley Kubrick of the early 1970s was at the apex of his fame and John Calley, of Warner Bros., was a fan. It was via Calley that Kubrick received a sweetheart deal from Warner's, which essentially allowed him to make what he wanted for as much as he wanted and on the schedule he wanted. Still, while we have seen above that there were several reasons to understand why Kubrick was drawn to a little-known work by a novelist almost exclusively known for a different tome (what fame, if any, Thackeray has to us today is primarily reliant on his *Vanity Fair*), one might imagine that several eyebrows were raised when a director whose rise was on the crest of films about our modern world and future announced that his next work was going to be a costume drama.

In retrospect, we can observe that Kubrick was on the wrong side of commercial history with this choice. The Movie Brat generation that was just making its first forays in the early 1970s made its mark by elevating B-movies to blockbusters. Coppola's *The Godfather* in 1972, William Friedkin's *The Exorcist* in 1973 (a film that was, as well as its sequel, offered to Kubrick), and Spielberg's *Jaws* in 1975 were all in genres that no one would have identified as highbrow, and their high production value and significant financial success were precursors to George Lucas inventing the modern movie franchise with *Star Wars* in 1977. While one can look to Kubrick's *2001* as the elevation of a genre that had largely been considered disreputable on screen prior to its release (there are exceptions, of course), Kubrick's narrative was far from the swashbuckling serial that Lucas regenerated on his own London soundstages nearly a decade later. The

Movie Brats did not come from the Kubrick-Altman school of generic perversion, but rather from the influence of the Hitchcocko-Hawksian school of analysis pioneered by *Cahiers du Cinema*'s writers, wherein the most banal of stories could be made into high art by the attention and artistry of a creative director.

Kubrick was too old for the Movie Brats, and too young for the European Art Cinema movement, and thus fits uncomfortably into cinematic histories of the era. While not literally *sui generis* (and we will probe some of Kubrick's cinematic influences later), he and his work are and were unique and do not fit into any "school" or easy grouping. *Barry Lyndon* itself lands on a marketplace hinge, when films of ideas gave way to films of sensation. Its commercial impact on the American moviescape was rather small, and despite its success across the pond, it is the only one of Kubrick's latter works to have not performed well at the box office in his country of origin.

Could it been a failure of casting? Ryan O'Neal was a star, having seen considerable success as the lead in *Love Story*. Kubrick himself was drawn to O'Neal after having repeatedly seen him in Peter Bogdanovich's screwball attempt *What's Up, Doc?*, which Kubrick's children enjoyed watching. O'Neal was, however, the only star in the film; Lady Lyndon was played by Marisa Berenson, who had mostly worked as a model aside from her bit part in *Cabaret* and a silent role in Luchino Visconti's *Death in Venice* (wherein she plays the mother of a doomed child in a costume drama heavily reliant upon the zoom lens). The cast was rounded out by European actors of limited notoriety in the United States, aside from Hardy Kruger.

It may seem insultingly reductive to remind the reader of the importance of casting to a film's success, but recall Herr quoting Kubrick as nearly equating *The Godfather*'s greatness as a film with the greatness of its *casting*. Few would impugn the acting credentials of the many European supporting players in *Barry Lyndon* (while Patrick Magee drew some criticism for going over-the-top in *Clockwork* – or, rather, Kubrick drew criticism for pushing him there, as his performance is clearly of a piece with the overall work – he is quite sedate in *Barry Lyndon*), but both O'Neal and Berenson have found critical knives pointed in their direction. If we are to believe Raphael, Kubrick himself was critical of Berenson's acting skills, though Raphael pointed out that the silences forced upon her character by her alleged futility at delivering dialogue enriched the characterization of Lady Lyndon (Raphael 160). Her silence and (and so far as we can see) lack of will in confronting Barry over his misdeeds indicate her (and, by extension her society) to be empty and superficial. (Ryan O'Neal somewhat ungenerously said Berenson was "just being herself" by playing a character that was "[o]verbred, vacuous, giggly, and lazy" [Schickel 168], though no giggling appears in the final cut.) O'Neal's performance is far more crucial. There are only a few scenes in which he does not appear, and he is at various times called upon to be charming, rambunctious, tender, courageous, fearful, skilled with the sword, brutal, and, at long last, merciful – in short, Redmond Barry's emotions are all-encompassing of the human experience. Regardless, viewers not in tune with the film's strategies find O'Neal painfully restrained (Pauline Kael going so far to refer to him as a "puppet" [Kael 49]). In fact, O'Neal exemplifies one of the polar opposites of Kubrick's leads: the stoic, outwardly unfeeling blank slate (the astronauts in *2001*, Joker in *Full Metal Jacket*, Tom Cruise's Bill Harford in *Eyes Wide Shut*) versus the stylized, big performances put on by showmen (Peter Sellers' turns in *Lolita* and *Strangelove*, George C. Scott in *Strangelove*, Malcolm McDowell in *A Clockwork Orange*, R. Lee Ermey and Vincent D'Onofrio in *Full Metal Jacket*, and, biggest of all, Jack Nicholson in *The Shining*). To try to erect an emotional epic on the foundation of such a tabula rasa as O'Neal's performance seems a curious choice for someone trying to emulate the wide-ranging appeal of *The Godfather*, with its vital, Method-trained faces.

But another view would be that O'Neal's blankness was a blessing. Redmond Barry's attitudes are often left opaque by O'Neal's performance, leaving The Narrator to fill in the gaps, but in fact this emotional evasiveness is endemic to the society into which Barry is attempting to insert himself. We shall see below how this performing style is situated within a narrative strategy learned from silent film, and one in which layers of commentary complement bare narrative: in *Barry Lyndon*, as in so many of his other works, Kubrick delivers a story and a critical attitude regarding it simultaneously.

Matching O'Neal's performance, not to mention the dry wariness of The Narrator, Barry himself is a blank slate. He presents himself to Lord Wendover (Andre Morell) as a pursuer of a peerage, and Wendover attempts to make Barry over in the image of a noble and prosperous man. Barry has drive and ambition, but he is largely devoid of convictions and principles, meaning that he has nothing to sacrifice (or so he thinks) as he works to increase his status (or, perhaps given the shallow frivolities cultivated by high society, we should say he *plays* to increase his status).

And it is difficult to credibly claim that O'Neal does not deliver in the film's most emotional passage, and perhaps the most openly emotional sequence in any Kubrick film (with the possible exception of the singing denouement of *Paths of Glory*), when his son Bryan (David Morley) dies from complications suffered in a horsing accident. This sequence will be discussed later, but the breaks in O'Neal's voice as he tries to get through a hyperbolic war story that he has told Bryan before are heartbreaking and authentic. As Barry's relationship with Bryan is a respite from his usual callousness and interpersonal depravity, so too in his scenes with Bryan do we find O'Neal at his best and most real; at every step, the performance *is* the character.

Aside from the casting of such a non-traditional lead, *Barry Lyndon*'s commercial reception was limited by the combination of its pacing and lack of the spectacular. Kubrick's pacing, from *Lolita* on, is often deliberate, but while *2001* can coast by on the strength of its unprecedented special effects, and *A Clockwork Orange* generates interest from its provocative sex and violence, *Barry Lyndon*'s most famous feature may be its arguably unmatched cinematic beauty, relying more on its technically and creatively impressive candlelight shooting – made possible by specially-configured Zeiss lenses that had been crafted for NASA – an appeal more subtle than the attractions of Kubrick's more genre-oriented works.

Kubrick himself hinted as much in his regular interview with Michel Ciment. Ciment, long-time editor of the French cinema journal *Positif*, was (along with *The Guardian*'s Alexander Walker) one of the few journalists allowed repeated audience with Kubrick. Ciment's critical volume on the director contains the series of interviews he conducted with him, one for each of his features from *A Clockwork Orange* through *Full Metal Jacket* (though in the latter case, the "interview" is a series of notes and commentary Kubrick submitted to Ciment as a substitute, perhaps fulfilling a fantasy Kubrick had once ascribed to Nabokov: "He would only agree to write down the answers and then send them to the interviewer who would write the questions" [Ciment 167].) He opens the interview regarding *Barry Lyndon* by observing that Kubrick had "given almost no interviews" on the film. Kubrick explains his approach to interviews thusly:

> What I generally manage to do is to discuss the background
> information connected with the story ... For example, with *Dr.
> Strangelove* I could talk about the spectrum of bizarre ideas
> connected with the possibilities of accidental or unintentional
> nuclear warfare. *2001: A Space Odyssey* allowed speculation
> about ultra-intelligent computers, life in the universe, and a whole
> range of science-fiction ideas. *A Clockwork Orange* involved law
> and order, criminal violence, authority versus freedom, etc. With
> *Barry Lyndon* you haven't got these topical issues to talk around,
> so I suppose that does make it a bit more difficult (ibid.).

In short, no one was writing newspaper editorials about Zeiss lenses. Kubrick's work from *Lolita* forward was met critically with a mix of enthusiasm and repudiation, which over time gave way to acceptance and canonization, some protests notwithstanding. The initial reaction to *Barry Lyndon* was no different, though perhaps there were a few more negative voices, while few of the positive ones were as enthusiastic as they had been for, say, *2001*. (Other filmmakers often seemed more open to Kubrick's films than the critics; Paul Schrader, in a *Film Comment* interview with Richard Thompson in 1976, declared *Lyndon* a "a revolutionary film, a slap in the face of the entire history of motion pictures. It's an important film. I have endless respect for it. Nobody quite knows what to think of it. It's an assault" [Thompson]. [It is interesting to note the diametric reactions from Schrader and his one-time mentor, longtime Kubrick opponent Pauline Kael. Kael derisively wondered if Kubrick hadn't been "schooling himself in late Dreyer and Bresson and Rossellini," thus turning the film "into a religious exercise" {Kael 49}. Schrader makes the same references, putting *Barry Lyndon* alongside his heroes {and book subjects} "Dreyer, Bresson, Ozu," along with "Rossellini, Boetticher," and others {Thompson}. Of course, for Schrader, this was cause for celebration.] Not all filmmakers necessarily agreed: Billy Wilder, though he went out of his way multiple times to praise Kubrick in conversation with Cameron Crowe, speaking admiringly of how "he trump[e]d the trump" with each new movie [Crowe 24, 215], did allow that *Barry Lyndon* was the only Kubrick picture he didn't like [23-24]. Well, nobody's perfect.)

The pace and tone are quite different from other picaresque period pieces of the era; moviegoers were more accustomed to the likes of *Tom Jones* and Richard Lester's *Musketeer* films (as well as his somewhat unfortunate George MacDonald Fraser adaptation *Royal Flash*, which like *Lyndon* was released in 1975, and starred in its title role one Malcolm McDowell). *Lyndon*'s more serious tone and measured pacing led some to consider it lifeless: Pauline Kael even had the gall to whine that the Handel sarabande served as "offputting" "embalming fluid" (Kael 50), that the "action sequences" "aren't meant to be exciting; they're meant only to be *visually* exciting" (ibid.) (as though visual excitement in a motion picture merits an "only"), and seemed personally offended that it lacked the pace and tone of *Tom Jones*. Kubrick may have had in mind certain virtues of another deliberately-paced and stentorian epic, but in lacking pulp appeal *Lyndon* had no chance of matching the cultural impact of *The Godfather*.

Even today, *Barry Lyndon* stands apart in Kubrick's filmography. Culturally iconic images abound from nearly all his films made from *Spartacus* forward, but *Lyndon* remains nearly unparodied and unimitated.

Nonetheless, the tide appears to be turning; in 2022's *Sight & Sound*/British Film Institute poll of directors and critics to rank the greatest film of all time, *Lyndon* ranked 45th (up from 59th in 2012) amongst the critics (only *2001* ranked higher, at 6th) and an impressive 12th (up from 19th in 2012) on the directors' list (*2001* ranked 1st). Perhaps more fans of The Big Movie are ready to be heard.

CHAPTER THREE
HELL'S ANGEL

CINEMA MAGAZINE IN 1963 printed a list of Stanley Kubrick's ten favorite films (Ciment 34). Some of the films and filmmakers are to be expected: Fellini, Bergman, Welles, and Chaplin make appearances, as do other luminaries and their films which are predecessors to some that Kubrick had made or would later make (Huston's *The Treasure of the Sierra Madre*'s climax prefigures that of *The Killing*, while Antonioni's *La Notte* – a tale of an upper-middle-class married couple confronting temptation at parties thrown by the idle rich – is a complement to *Eyes Wide Shut*). Big performers and performances are listed: Olivier as Henry V, WC Fields in *The Bank Dick*.

Two of the films are more startling: William Wellman's *Roxie Hart* and Howard Hughes' *Hell's Angels*. Wellman's film is best-known to viewers today as being an early telling of the story later brought to the musical stage by Bob Fosse as *Chicago*; the satirical edge of the story may certainly have appealed to the side of Kubrick that conjured *Strangelove* (and the film also features Adolphe Menjou, a key figure in *Paths of Glory*). As for *Hell's Angels*, Kubrick's widow Christiane confessed to *Sight & Sound*'s Nick James after the director's passing that he "loved to see any dumb film with a fight between aeroplanes ... [h]e didn't want the plot, he just wanted to see if there was a good fight between planes" (James 18). Obviously, *Hell's Angels* would fit that bill, but there is, perhaps, something else that struck the young Kubrick's fancy.

This is the opening shot of *Barry Lyndon*:

And, nearly thirteen minutes into *Hell's Angels*, we have this shot:

Identical? No. Reminiscent? Certainly.

Kubrick's cinema is distinctive in so many ways that it may seem odd to point to particular points of influence, though occasionally his detractors have gleefully done so, as though such observation might impugn his reputation. Godard, for instance, classified Kubrick's tracking shots in *The Killing* as "glacial copies of Ophuls'" (Godard 202) (Ophuls was an admitted influence on Kubrick, and one Kubrick was never shy about proclaiming, and it may be worth noting that this passage by Godard contains the single richest line in the history of film criticism, wherein the director of *Les Carabiniers* and future director of *Film Socialisme* and *Goodbye to Language* says that *Lolita* proves that "Kubrick need not abandon the cinema provided he films characters who exist instead of ideas which exist only in the bottom drawers of old scriptwriters who believe that the cinema is the seventh art" [ibid.]). Of course, no filmmaker has truly made films in a vacuum, and resonances can be felt in any picture. Kubrick was a sponge of films, and constantly inquisitive in seeking out the "secrets" of the makers of the films he admired. Stories abound from filmmakers who were phoned by Kubrick, or even (though more rarely) encountered by him in person, and were asked questions as to how certain effects or performances were achieved. Cinematographer Vilmos Zsigmond, who shot Robert Altman's *McCabe & Mrs. Miller*, reported that Altman had told him of encountering Kubrick at a London theater, where Altman had gone to see *2001* and Kubrick *McCabe*. Running into each other in the lobby, "Kubrick started to ask Altman questions," particularly about how he achieved his noted pan-and-zooms (Schaefer and Salvato 317).

The zoom, of course, went on to become one of the most striking visual hallmarks of *Barry Lyndon*, though Kubrick's zooms are far more linear than Altman's (he does, rarely, such as in the introduction of the character of Lord Wendover, have his camera pan or tilt to adjust the composition during a zoom, but such adjustments, when they appear, are minute). The zoom was a relatively new addition to the art of fictional moviemaking in general as well as to Kubrick's style; he had used zooms to some extent before (singling out Kirk Douglas during the ill-fated attack on The Ant Hill in *Paths of Glory*, pulling back from Humbert Humbert's lustful eyes to reveal hula-hooping Lolita, the crash zooms detailing instrument panels aboard Major Kong's B-52, and to unveil a trick shot aboard *2001*'s Discovery), but it was with *A Clockwork Orange* that Kubrick began the pattern of opening scenes zooming out of a detail to show a larger whole; the opening shot of the film starts with the iconic and startling close-up of Malcolm McDowell, and slowly both zooms out and tracks back to reveal the bizarre Milk Bar in which he sits.

The usage in *Barry Lyndon* becomes almost pathological. Though the film does not open with a zoom, one opens the third scene (and first with dialogue), and we have continual usage throughout the film, only pared back when, as we shall see, the pace of the story needs to accelerate. Kubrick is so dedicated to this device that, in more than one candle-lit scene, the camera actually pushes into or pulls away from its subjects in *imitation* of a zoom.

The other striking, and much-discussed, element of this film's visual style was the reliance upon specially-modified Zeiss lenses that had been developed for NASA use, allowing Kubrick and Alcott to shoot scenes entirely by candlelight. The limitations of these lenses altered Kubrick's standard visual strategy and renders this film somewhat anomalous in his oeuvre.

The two Zeiss lenses were prime lenses, one with an effective focal length of 36.5mm and the other of 50mm. These are normal-length lenses that would be used on most 35mm film productions; but Stanley Kubrick was not a standard director. For the bulk of his career, whether through the influence of Orson Welles or his own photojournalist experience, Kubrick favored wide-angle lenses, even in close-ups and medium shots, where the standard would be to use a longer lens, creating a flatter image that is more flattering to the actors (Shelley Duvall reported in a documentary segment on John Alcott [*Six Kinds of Light: John Alcott*] that the cinematographer would often ask Kubrick to use longer lenses for close-ups in *The Shining*, only to be shot down), and Larry Smith, an electrician on Alcott's crew on this film who moved up to lighting cameraman for *Eyes Wide Shut*, reported that much of the latter film was shot at 18mm and only rarely did they use any lens longer than 35mm (Pizzello). Even as far back as *The Killing*, in effect Kubrick's first professional film, the director quarreled with his director of photography, the veteran Lucien Ballard, over his choice to use 25mm lenses – particularly wide for the time – for panning and tracking shots, as Ballard objected to the distortion derived from such lenses – certainly the effect Kubrick was intending (LoBrutto 118).

Wide-angle lenses are prominent throughout most Kubrick films, as are the tracking shots he is also known for. Under Ophuls' influence, Kubrick's early films demonstrate an enthusiasm for a mobile camera that can even transcend walls, and in *Lolita* – Kubrick's most Ophulsian film in nearly every respect, with its treatment of tragic love, not to mention the casting of urbane two-time Ophuls star James Mason – it can glide up and down stairs and in and out of rooms. The exigencies of *Strangelove* and *2001* limited his use of such shots (in fact, there is very little forward visual momentum in the latter film *until* the stars break for the Stargate sequence, again a likely intended effect), but in *A Clockwork Orange* Kubrick synthesized the visual style that would dominate the last stage of his career: wide lenses, low angles, lateral and tunnel tracking shots (he no longer practiced the gliding diagonal moving camera of Ophuls and *Lolita*), scenes established with slow zoom-outs (this lessened in his final two pictures, particularly *Eyes Wide Shut*), and the occasional use of a crash zoom for a shock effect.

In preparing the Zeiss lenses for *Barry Lyndon*, he *did* try to go wider; Ed DiGiulio, the consultant who prepared the lenses, told *American Cinematographer* that they had also developed a lens with the focal length of 24mm, but in tests "Kubrick determined that the lens gave a bit too much distortion, so that he would not wish to intercut photography from this lens with photography from the other two" (DiGiulio). Though the special lenses were only used for a handful of scenes, the decision to not intercut wildly different focal lengths pervades the whole film. Kubrick uses normal-length lenses throughout, and in close-ups, the blurrier background that results gives the shots the feeling of period portraiture. (Alcott did inform Ciment that he used 22mm lenses for interiors in the film [Ciment 216], though even so they are certainly used less frequently, as a percentage matter, than similar focal lengths in Kubrick's other work, and he further reported a relative absence of the usually ubiquitous 18mm, a glaring absence particularly noticeable in close-ups.)

Another limitation of the Zeiss lenses was depth of field; the very shallow range of focus meant that actors posed by candlelight could not be mobile lest they fall out of focus. Though Kubrick was always very precise with his compositions, the lack of movement also severely limited the use of the tracking shots, and they appear scarcely in this film; in concert with the longer lenses, this provides the film with a unique visual signature among Kubrick's work. The stationary nature of many characters contributes to the sense of the film being a series of carefully-composed paintings, an element of delight to its many fans and of consternation to Kubrick's enemies. The aforementioned zoom also contributes to this sense. Many writers have attempted to describe the zoom's effect, some concluding that it represents standing near to a painting and slowly backing away from it, others that it represents the pulling back from a detail of history to reveal its larger pictures, others that it situates the characters as small pieces in a world and fate that overwhelms them. In fact, most scholars say all of these things, as they are not contradictory, and all certainly seem appropriate.

But another result of the zoom's use is that it delays the release of information, and control of information is integral to the film's structure, both visual and narrative (as though "visual" and "narrative" can be separated in a Kubrick picture) – in addition to its delays, the film also frequently provides information *earlier* than is typical in dramatic presentation. The most striking aural exemplar of this fluid approach to the dissemination of information is The Narrator sardonically and sonorously voiced by Michael Hordern. In one of the film's most curious strategies, The Narrator frequently informs us as to the conclusion of events right before they happen, completely removing from the viewer the element of surprise and investing instead the experience of suspense.

Kubrick spoke about this directly with Michel Ciment, drawing a parallel between our being "told that ... Bryan is going to die at the same time we watch [Barry and Bryan] playing happily together" and the "dramatic effect" of having "the knowledge that the *Titanic* is doomed while you watch carefree scenes of preparation and departure." He further asserted that "*Barry Lyndon* is a story which does not depend upon surprise" (Ciment 170-171).

The narration finds its source in Thackeray's novel, though its use is very different. In both serial and novel forms, the narrative is presented as the memoir of a braggadocios fool, and the reader must deduce that the narrator is self-serving and unreliable (the original, serialized form of the novel included an editor who would chime in to dispute Barry's claims from time to time). Kubrick, having just made a film presented from the point of view of its unreliable narrator, rejected that approach here, telling Ciment "[i]t might have worked as a comedy by the juxtaposition of Barry's version of the truth with the reality on the screen, but I don't think that *Barry Lyndon* should have been done as a comedy" (170).

Kubrick's decision to maintain the voiceover technique, while relocating it from Barry to an unseen and allegedly impartial observer, allows him to condense exposition but still provide "ironic counterpoint," as he put it about the sequence where a romantic idyll between Barry and Lischen (Diana Koerner), a peasant German woman, is undercut by The Narrator's snide gossip about the high turnover of her bed. This control of the release of information is key, and in speaking to Ciment, Kubrick betrayed a bit of his own strategy of using image, performance, and voiceover narration to create a cohesive whole (still in discussion of the Lischen sequence): "You could have had Barry give signals to the audience, through his performance, indicating that he is really insincere and opportunistic, but this would be unreal. When we try to deceive we are convincing as we can be, aren't we?" (ibid.)

Thus Kubrick can dramatize scenes on multiple planes: the external, superficial reality of the situation (Barry and Lischen's outwardly sincere emoting and claims of "Ich liebe dich") is presented along with the internal, truthful reality of their inner attitudes (using each other for temporary physical affection). Central to this is an understanding that people do not always speak their true feelings or even behave according to them, and in fact the high society to which Barry aspires has its own sets of codes and mores in which contempt and dismissal can be concealed by politesse and ritual. Body language, spoken language, voiceover, and, indeed, the musical score all work together to present the entire picture – as though we had started with one detail (Barry and Lischen's expressions of affection) and zoomed out to gain a complete understanding of the encounter.

The opening duel image is accompanied by The Narrator informing us, in perfect synchronization with the firing pistols, that we are seeing Barry's father be killed, and that the dispute that led to the duel regarded "the purchase of some horses." This subtly sets up the first of the film's many rhymes – the purchase of a horse leads to the death of Barry's father (opening a gap in his life that he continually attempts to fill, from Captain Grogan to Potzdorf to the Chevalier), and the purchase of a horse leads also to the death of his son (opening a gap that is never adequately filled).

Shortly, we find another scene echoed in the film's climax; after a slow pan – slow pans are another frequent establishing technique deployed throughout the film – revealing a suitor walking alongside Barry's mother (Marie Kean) while The Narrator informs us that she dedicated herself to the raising of her son in lieu of remarrying, we cut to an erotically-charged game of cards between Barry and his first love, his cousin Nora Brady (Gay Hamilton). After the film's climactic duel, Barry plays cards with his mother while he recuperates. While not erotically charged, the relationship between Barry and his mother bears traces of a coupling in other emotional ways; the mother is protective of Barry before he leaves home, but then also plays the Lady Macbeth role of urging him along his attempted path to a peerage. As Barry's marriage and sobriety dissolve after Bryan's death, it is his mother who takes on the responsibility of caring for him and the estate; the introduction of the mother before the introduction of Nora implies the primary influence she will continue to have on her son's life. (Interestingly, the first words spoken by Napoleon [in voice-over] in Kubrick's last draft for that picture [dated September of 1969] are "My mother has always loved me. She would do anything for me" [Kubrick 1]. The opening scene shows his mother telling the four-year-old Napoleon a bedtime story, in anticipation of the bedtime story told by Barry to Bryan one two occasions; the script closes on a scene of Napoleon's mother surveying his childhood possessions.)

Barry's failure to successfully woo Nora establishes for him his life goal: to ascend to higher society and live the life of a gentleman; it is John Quin's (Leonard Rossiter) status as a landowner that wins him the hand of Nora, not any affection on her part. Even before the affair's resolution, The Narrator advises us of Barry's envy for the splendor of the military company that Quin commands. (We slowly zoom *in* to Barry as this is said, in opposition to the standard zoom-out, as instead of moving from the specific to the general, we move from the general to the specific – the inner thoughts of Barry. This zoom-in is answered by another later in the film as Barry laments being in the army, another example of a structural echo.) Nora's brothers repeatedly refer to the "fifteen hundred a year" the marriage to Quin would bring into the Brady family, and Grogan reminds Barry that Nora's father has debts that will be solved by the union.

Barry's relationship with Grogan is one of his most tender, and the first instance we see of his search for a father figure. The staging and editing of their initial conversation establishes the difference between Barry's relationship with Grogan, which has actual commonality and devotion, and his relationship with Nora, which is empty and superficial. After Nora dances with Quin, we have a two-handed scene between Barry and Nora wherein he complains to her of her refusal to dance with him instead. The camera is fixed in longshot as Barry and Nora approach (we do not get the tracking shot we might expect of Kubrick here). They reach an impasse, and part ways. The dialogue Barry and Grogan have after Barry has thrown a glass in Quin's face at the news of his engagement to Nora is initially shot in a very similar way, in a long two-shot. However, the impasse here is bridged, and after Barry expresses his dedication to Nora, Grogan replies that Barry is "after [his] own soul" – on which line we cut into a closer two-shot, which is maintained for the balance of the scene, where Grogan tells Barry that so long as he lives, Barry will "never be in want of a friend." The camera draws closer as the men do, a closeness deprived Barry in his relationship to Nora, and in the camera's presentation of it.

Throughout this opening sequence, and the film as a whole, much of what we learn about Barry comes from what other people – and not just The Narrator – say. The Narrator's role in conveying Barry's thoughts and attitudes is obvious, but the narration's interaction with the images that accompany them is more subtle. In one early image, after Barry's argument with Nora, we cut to him chopping firewood, and a zoom-out displays Barry alone, dwarfed by the horizon; The Narrator speaks of Barry's futile resolve to avoid seeing or thinking about Nora – allowing the audience to infer that his wood-chopping represents an outlet for his romantic and sexual frustration as much as (or more than) it might be a necessary chore. This constructive effect is reminiscent of the famed Kuleshov Effect, wherein identical shots of an expressionless actor are intercut with prompts of varying emotional import (some joyous, some tragic), fooling viewers into thinking the actor is presenting a wide range of emotional responses, when in fact such responses are being implanted in the audience by the juxtaposition of the images. The only film theory that seems to have had any impact on Kubrick was that of Pudovkin (though he had read but not "really understood" Eisenstein [Gelmis 315]), so he was certainly familiar with montage theory, and in fact had utilized constructive editing throughout his career, often in scenes of violence – one fight scene in his mostly amateurish debut, *Fear and Desire*, is a series of cuts of men *starting* to punch and then the indirect *results* of the strike, such as the victim clutching tightly to some loaf of bread; HAL's murder of the astronaut Frank Poole in *2001* is similar, as we never see the floating pod actually have an impact on its victim, but cut from a close-up of the pod to Poole floating helplessly and hopelessly through space: the viewer is invited to combine the images seen into an understanding of another, unseen, image.

These expositional strategies are clearly reminiscent of those of silent film, a resemblance Kubrick happily proclaimed, gleefully admitting as much to Michel Ciment when it was mentioned to him. "I think silent films got a lot more things right than talkies," he said (Ciment 174). The point was important enough that Kubrick, unprompted by Ciment, brought it up again five years later in relation to *The Shining*, and his comments also provide a guide to the director's approach here:

> I think that the scope and flexibility of movie stories would be greatly enhanced by borrowing something from the structure of silent movies where points that didn't require weight could be presented by a shot and a title card. Something like: *Title: 'Billy's uncle'. Picture: Uncle giving Billy ice cream.* In a few seconds, you would introduce Billy's uncle and say something about him without being burdened with a scene. This economy of statement gave silent movies a much greater narrative scope and flexibility than we have today. In my view, there are very few sound films, including those regarded as masterpieces, which could not be presented almost as effectively on the stage, assuming a good set, the same cast and quality of performances. You couldn't do that with a great silent movie (187).

The voice-over and third-party dialogue thus take on the role of audible silent film title cards (and, in fact, many silent movie theaters employed "lecturers" to provide explanatory verbal accompaniment to the visuals [Aumont 7]). Even the cutting pattern of scenes allows for important dialogue spoken by others to accompany shots of Barry, and other characters frequently pick up the slack when The Narrator is silent. When Barry interrupts a romantic idyll between Quin and Nora, the camera focuses on Barry even as Nora's brothers complain to him, only cutting to them when absolutely necessary. After Barry throws the glass into Quin's face, the confused father of Nora is told by one of his sons what Barry's motivation is, as Barry silently glares at Quin. After the staged duel with Quin, that same brother discusses with Barry's mother the boy's future – the bulk of the conversation, *about* Barry, is staged as a three-shot where Barry sits silently between the interlocutors, as though their conversation is a voice-over explaining his options; only when Barry speaks do we cut into a more conventional coverage of a shot-reverse shot between Barry and his mother for their short conversation. And not long thereafter, once Barry's assets are stolen and he is in a desperate strait, an army soldier's recruitment speech focuses on the speaker for most of his pitch – but the only cuts to Barry accompany lines in the speech ("All clever young fellows who are free and able and are ambitious of becoming gentlemen" and "Those meeting the qualifications will immediately receive his majesty's royal bounty of one-and-a-half guineas") which refer specifically to him.

Speaking to Ciment, Kubrick likened these silent film techniques to the efficiency of storytelling in "the best TV commercials" (Ciment 187), a theme he would repeat in further interviews. Promoting *Full Metal Jacket* to *Rolling Stone*'s Tim Cahill in 1987, Kubrick made similar comments, but also allowed that he "suppose[d] there's really nothing that would substitute for the great dramatic moment, fully played out" (Cahill 375). *Barry Lyndon* has its share of this sort of presentation, as well, though the unconventionally inert performance of Ryan O'Neal upset some viewers and also runs the risk of making the character seem passive.

As alluded to above, *Barry Lyndon* comes in the middle of a curious back-and-forth in the dynamism of Kubrick's leading men. Very few characters are allowed the large performances that hallmarked *A Clockwork Orange* – Leonard Rossiter as Captain Quin, Frank Middlemass in the tiny role of Sir Charles Lyndon, and arguably at points Leon Vitali as Lord Bullingdon are the only exceptions. Big performances would contradict the stable, ordered high society that comprises the milieu of the film: decorum rules the day, even when characters find themselves in opposition.

Beyond the fairly affectless performances being appropriate to the film's historical and societal setting, they also, of course, contribute to the effectiveness of the application of the silent film strategies discussed above. O'Neal as Barry is frequently a manifestation of the actor in Kuleshov's experiments; and the times where he is *not*, and is asked to overtly emote, such as when he meets the Chevalier or sits vigil at Bryan's deathbed, gain all the more significance for their break from the film's otherwise established patterns.

The music also plays a role in establishing character moods and creating further audio echoes; the dinner scene which climaxes with the thrown glass is a dry run for the card-playing seduction scene between Barry and Lady Lyndon near the end of the first half of the film. Even before the engagement between Quin and Nora is announced, we have a story told entirely in glances between a desperate Barry, an elfish Nora, and a smug Quin – all while the soundtrack plays The Chieftains' arrangement of the Irish folk tune "Women of Ireland", which heretofore has represented the "love theme" for Barry and Nora, just as the latter glances among Barry, Lady Lyndon, and a scolding Reverend Runt (Murray Melvin) are accompanied by the Barry-Lady Lyndon "love theme" of the Schubert Trio.

The film's opening theme is a dramatic orchestration of a sarabande by Handel, which in itself is a small tweak to the melody of the traditional Spanish dance tune *La folia*. It is perhaps this resonance that struck Kubrick who, upon initially hearing the tune played on a classical guitar, was reminded of Ennio Morricone (Ciment 175). (Sergio Leone told the tale of Kubrick calling him and saying, "I've got all Ennio Morricone's albums. Can you explain to me why I only seem to like the music he composed for *your* films?" "Don't worry," Leone said that Leone said, "I didn't think much of Richard Strauss until I saw *2001!*" [Frayling 299]) The evocation of Morricone may be why Kubrick elected to use a stripped-down arrangement of the piece for both duel sequences, the first of which is the (unbeknownst to us or Barry) arranged duel with Quin in which the older man's death will be staged, thus removing Barry from the picture so that the captain can marry Nora unencumbered. The musical arrangement adds tension to the scene, but also undercuts the majestic beauty of the duel's setting, introduced to us by a zoom out from a pistol being loaded to present a larger landscape that dwarfs the foolish mortals quarreling over an impertinent flirt. This is the film in microcosm, of course, and Kubrick's cinema at large, a presentation of human folly in the shadow of an unconcerned natural order. ("The most terrifying fact about the universe is not that it is hostile but that it is indifferent," Kubrick once said [Nordern 353].)

This worldview threatens to combine with the "silent film" expositional techniques to render the participants passive, enslaved to fate (The Narrator even refers to "fate" in nearly anthropomorphic terms multiple times, and also refers to "death" in a similar manner as Bryan draws close to his last breath), but the true lesson of Kubrick's tragedies is that man creates his own fate through his imperfect plans and self-centered action. We see this pattern already with Barry in his early days, as his reckless pursuit of Nora creates enemies who easily trick him, and we see it in his final push to ruin, as his pursuit of a title drains his family's financial resources, and his inability to hold back his temper leads directly to his excommunication from society. The luck of Barry Lyndon is bad indeed, but that is luck borne of his own flaws, just as Kubrick's cinema dramatizes that human ruin comes from the shortcomings of human nature. The next steps on Barry's path take him even closer to the heart of human brutality.

CHAPTER FOUR
PATHS OF GLORY

TO BE FAIR TO Barry, the misfortune that costs him his money and his father's sword and pistols can't be laid entirely at his feet, though perhaps he was a bit reckless exposing his coins when unknowingly encountering a notorious highwayman and his son at a roadstop eatery. Barry's robbery at the hands of Captain Feeny is an invention of Kubrick's (expanding on a minor character in the novel), and an example of the streamlining and telescoping of the novel's events he needed to undertake.

When Kubrick submitted his screenplay to Warner Bros. and showed it to prospective collaborators in early 1973, he, out of fear that the identity of his public domain source material might be leaked and exploited by some other filmmaker, disguised the bulk of the character names and the novel's title. (Redmond Barry's pseudonym of "Roderick James" might serve as a cheeky reference to another picaresque novel, Tobias Smollet's 1748 *The Adventures of Roderick Random*.) This version of the screenplay hews closer to the novel in several respects (it maintains the voiceover in Barry's voice, for instance), and dramatizes Thackeray's scenario in which Barry makes it all the way to Dublin before falling prey to con artists. This extended sequence takes up approximately eight of the screenplay's 114 pages, a stunning amount of time to dedicate to the simple narrative function of separating Barry from his money. (It is also worth noting that this document was *not* used as the shooting script; instead, Kubrick proceeded with what amounted to an outline of scenes, using the novel's pages as a basis for constructing the scenes he had selected and invented [LoBrutto 377]; as an illustration, the entirety of the scripted matter for the climactic duel with Bullingdon was "Barry duels with Lord Bullingdon" [405].)

The encounter with the highwayman Feeny also continues the conceit of a polite verbal veneer masking sinister intent, though, in this case, with pistols drawn and demands made, there is no attempt to disguise Feeny's nature – he is even sufficiently notorious that Barry is familiar with his name.

Kubrick raids his *Napoleon* screenplay here to add pathos; while in the novel, Barry does speak to carrying his father's sword and pistols, here he loses them to Feeny's theft. Barry unsuccessfully pleads for them on a sentimental basis. Kubrick utilized a similar device early in *Napoleon*; Bonaparte's men have seized all the weapons from Paris' citizenry, and Josephine's teenage son comes to Napoleon personally to lobby for the return of his father's sword (Kubrick 32-33). Napoleon's return of the item leads to his meeting and romancing Josephine; here, the loss of the item – and twenty gold guineas, sufficient to fool Feeny into presuming Barry is "a well set-up gentleman" – leads Barry to the state where he can finally live the dreams of glory that had filled him with envy when he watched Quin and his men.

Thus Kubrick returns to one of his favorite settings: the military and war. He had begun his feature career with a highly metaphorical and putatively poetic war film in *Fear and Desire* (his preferred title was *The Shape of Fear*, though the neophyte director had not yet achieved the professional status to control the terms of his film's release), and many consider *Paths of Glory* his first great film. The spectacle of cinematic battle always intrigued Kubrick – his childhood friend (and future director) Alexander Singer reports that he was so taken by the battle on the ice in Eisenstein's *Alexander Nevsky* that he played the Prokofiev score over and over until his sister broke his record (LoBrutto 56). Eisenstein's staging the build-up to the battle significantly informed Kubrick's treatment of the climactic battle in *Spartacus*, a production which otherwise seemed to give him little lasting joy. The geometry of large battles seemed to excite Kubrick for their compositional possibilities: his screenplay for *Napoleon* featured several sequences in which military strategy and the movement of vast armies would be illustrated with animated maps, and he told Joseph Gelmis that "from a purely schematic point of view, Napoleonic battles are so beautiful, like vast lethal ballets" (Gelmis 296).

Beyond the spectacle, Kubrick found a particular dramatic interest in the plight of a soldier. "One of the attractions of a war or crime story," he said in 1959, "is that it provides an almost unique opportunity to contrast an individual [...] with a a solid framework of accepted value, which [...] can be used as a counterpoint to a human, individual, emotional situation" (Young 6). "Attitudes crystallize and come into the open." So though Kubrick had an interest in war as a phenomenon (John Milius said, "He was endlessly fascinated by honor and valor, the regimental esprit de corps" [Bogdanovich]), he was also interested in it as a fulcrum for other thematic expressions for which war and military matters provided a suitable dramatic backdrop. Though *Paths of Glory* was seen as sufficiently anti-military to earn a ban in France and France-friendly countries, Kubrick scholar and confidante Alexander Walker located the film's concern as being about a "deeper conflict" "between the leaders and the led. It exists whether there is a war or not, but a war situation widens the division fatally [...] [the film] is more pertinently an illustration of war as the continuation of a class struggle" (Walker 69). In much the same way, *Full Metal Jacket* isn't so much about the Vietnam War specifically as it is, per Kubrick's co-screenwriter Michael Herr, "how you put into a film or a book the living, behaving presence of what Jung called the Shadow" (Herr FMJ). The Shadow of *Full Metal Jacket* somehow casts itself back through time to the early military scenes of *Barry Lyndon*. Upon being inducted into his regiment, Barry quickly finds himself in a verbal altercation with a large, powerful soldier named Toole (played by Pat Roach, a frequent stuntman who was defeated by Dr. Indiana Jones in both *Raiders of the Lost Ark* and *Indiana Jones and the Temple of Doom* – and, as a villainous henchman in *Willow*, played a character named for one of Kubrick's primary nemeses – he played General Kael). Barry's gentlemanly aspirations are subtly reflected in his complaints about a greasy soup cup, complaints mocked by Toole and laughed at by other soldiers. Another soldier cues Barry with taunts regarding Toole's wife, and the verbal parrying is similar to Joker's first meeting of the larger and stronger Animal Mother in the latter film. The conflict here is resolved with fisticuffs, Barry defeating his larger opponent in a boxing match by using his speed and wits. Kubrick and O'Neal were both boxing fans, even watching video of fights together while on set (LoBrutto 397), and likely enjoyed shooting the sequence, but the narrative importance here is to establish Barry's resourcefulness and fearlessness in the face of long odds.

On a formal level, the boxing match is shot with a handheld camera (by Kubrick himself), a technique used only a few times in this film and relatively infrequently across Kubrick's work as a whole. Here, the handheld combines physical intimacy with a sense of lack of control, and it will return in Barry's next big fistfight, when he attacks Lord Bullingdon after the younger man insults him during a family musical recital. Barry is trained by his military experiences to respond to provocation with violence, and his tutelage in the rod while he is in the Prussian service establishes for him the punishment technique he imposes on a young Bullingdon on multiple occasions. The resonances between the military problem-solving/punishments and those Barry takes with him into domestic life illustrate his unsuitability for maintaining the "life of a gentleman" to which he so ardently aspires (and also satisfied Kubrick's clear attraction to narrative echoes and repetitions, more readily apparent in *A Clockwork Orange* and *Eyes Wide Shut*, both of which, in close adaptation of their source material, prominently feature the protagonist returning to the sites and characters of previous scenes in new contexts).

Yet the most important development for Barry during his time in the military is his brief reunion with and subsequent loss of Captain Grogan. Grogan offers Barry money and gives him the truth, and is immediately slain in battle. Grogan is played by Godfrey Quigley, who four years earlier had played the prison chaplain in *A Clockwork Orange*, and Kubrick went out of his way in interviews to praise his performance in the earlier film, telling Michel Ciment that "a very delicate balance had to be achieved in Godfrey's performance between his somewhat comical image and the important ideas he is called upon to express," ideas that substantiated "the moral voice of the film" (Ciment 149). This period of Kubrick's career, focused on stories set in Britain, must have pleased him greatly insofar as he got to work with British actors, whom he largely admired for their professionalism. Oft-told is the story of his noticing Charles Laughton and Laurence Olivier mumbling to themselves between scenes on the set of *Spartacus*; fearing that they were complaining about him, Kubrick took an opportunity to sneak behind them – only to learn that they were practicing their lines.

Knowledge of lines was of paramount importance to Kubrick, and he assigned his reputation of demanding many takes to the fact that actors frequently didn't know their lines. But, by this, he did not simply mean memorization, but a thorough comprehension and internalization of the lines. Matthew Modine reported that Kubrick had told him of Jack Nicholson:

> Jack would come in during the blocking and he kind of fumbled through the lines. He'd be learning them while he was there. And then you'd start shooting and after take three or take four or take five you'd get the Jack Nicholson that everybody knows and most directors would be happy with. And then you'd go up to 10 or 15 and he'd be really awful and then he'd start to understand what the lines were, what the lines meant, and then he'd become unconscious about what he was saying. So by take 30 or take 40 the lines became something else (Bogdanovich).

While the circumstances of the shooting and settings of *A Clockwork Orange* and *Barry Lyndon* leant themselves to a common casting pool to some degree, it is notable nonetheless that in these two films we see the most repetition of performers: aside from Quigley, Anthony Sharp appears in both films (as the Minister of the Interior in the earlier film, and as a "former minister" in the later), along with Patrick Magee, Steven Berkoff, and Philip Stone – who five years later, would become one of only two performers to work with Kubrick three times when he appeared in *The Shining* (tying Joe Turkel, who after a very small role in *The Killing* played one of the doomed soldiers in *Paths of Glory*, and then the ghostly bartender Lloyd in *The Shining*). Leonard Rossiter did not appear in *A Clockwork Orange*, but did in *2001* – which was of course also shot in England. Though Kubrick often worked with some of the biggest stars in movies, he was unafraid to work with less-known names. In a draft of his production notes for *Napoleon*, Kubrick said that "sufficient proof exists to demonstrate once and for all that the idea of loading up a film with many expensive names as protection against failure is not a viable idea [...] The only reason to use stars is when the star happens to be the best actor you can find for the part" (Castle 88). His final draft took a more financial tack, saying "over-priced movie stars do little besides leaving an insufficient amount of money to make the film properly, or cause an unnecessarily high picture cost," going on to cite a *Variety* study on the poor financial returns of films employing expensive stars (101). For as artistically inspired as the director was, he was also a keen businessman (and, per Michael Herr, "a terrible man to do business with, *terrible*" [Herr]). Stories abound of his attention to the details of marketing, advertising (even making sure that print ads were the right size and listed all available showings), and distribution (keeping lists of theaters and the business they did individually) – and, after all was said in done, his top two choices for Napoleon were David Hemmings and Oskar Werner, stars of the arthouse, and for Josephine his only choice was no less a star than Audrey Hepburn (Kubrick did eventually succeed in casting Werner in *Barry Lyndon* as Captain Potzdorf, though he replaced him with Hardy Kruger, apparently for reasons related to alcohol). In a fashion typical of his protagonists, however, Kubrick's detailed and careful plans were imperfect: he thought that *Barry Lyndon* would gross "nine figures" (Schickel 167) at the box office, but its worldwide figures, according to the Internet Movie Database, were "merely" $31.5 million (which, given the long tail of its home media distribution, should have been sufficient for the film to break even for Warners, as short as that figure may have been of the director's hopes).

While Kubrick's plans to make (or expand) a fortune with *Barry Lyndon* fell short, Redmond Barry's goal of making his way into gentlemanly society falls into peril after Grogan's death. It is here that we echo in reverse the previous zoom-in, here with Barry by the campfire, mourning his fate as The Narrator tells us that "Barry's thoughts turned from those of military glory to those of finding a way to escape the service." (This brief but crucial image is another "theft" from the Napoleon script, there used as Napoleon despairs over the silence and [suspected, by him, and known, to us] infidelity of Josephine [Kubrick 43]. In fact, a review of Kubrick's archives reveals that this shot's pose and composition derives from a piece of Napoleonic art, a rendering by Felicien von Myrbach-Rheinfeld of Jean-Roch Coignet, one of Napoleon's military staff [Ljujić 252-253].) The music heard is a Chieftains piece from earlier in the film, linking Barry's sadness about Grogan to his now comparatively idyllic background. Whereas Barry's jealous gaze upon the soldiers in all their finery in the film's opening minutes was portrayed in a shot showing him looking from left to right, his vigil by the fire is shot with him looking right to left. Michael Klein points out that this is a pattern throughout the film, where scenes of Barry's progress show him moving or looking from left-to-right, and scenes demonstrating his decline and fall show him moving or looking right-to-left (Klein). (See also the progression of Bryan's carriage during his birthday party vs. its direction during his funeral.)

Luckily for Barry, the next scenes resume the left-to-right movement. After we learn of Barry's intention of leaving the army, we see him and other soldiers pillaging a farmhouse (another image cribbed from *Napoleon* [Kubrick 46] and also somewhat styled on a specific piece of Napoeleonic art [Ljujić 253]) while The Narrator opines that "Gentlemen may talk of the age of chivalry, but remember the ploughmen, poachers, and pickpockets whom they lead. It is with these sad instruments that your great warriors and kings have been doing their murderous work in the world." Immediately we see Barry engage in craven dishonesty: an instance of the images, voiceover, and narrative all working in concert. Barry's next left-to-right approach is to a river and, as The Narrator tells us even before it happens, he finds a way out of the service "in a most singular manner." This short scene, in which Barry witnesses two homosexual soldiers in a river and overhears their conversation, learning that one is being sent on a courier mission, a mission which Barry then assumes under that soldier's name, is another condensation invented by the director. In the novel and the earlier script draft, Barry and the soldier he ultimately impersonates both encounter Lischen while the other is wounded. The sequence, on paper, has the potential for comic zaniness that those who wanted this film to be *Tom Jones* likely expected, where Lieutenant Fakenham (played by Jonathan Cecil), plays up his wounds and boorishly flirts with Lischen, only to grow frustrated at Barry's success with her. Indeed, Kubrick initially shot the sequence in this fashion, but, unsatisfied, dismissed Cecil with the promise that he would bring him back. Months later, he returned to shoot the altered version of the scene (LoBrutto 394).

The change serves multiple purposes. It severely shortens the action by which Barry deserts the army, four pages in the 1973 script, to a brief scene. It allows the Barry-Lischen sequence to play out on its own, without interference from another character, allowing it (apparent) tenderness. (It is also the first time we see – or at least see it implied – that Barry goes to bed with a woman, an event that took place with another character in the original Dublin con-artist sequence referenced above.) It also introduces, briefly, the theme of homosexuality to the movie (a theme that pops up in Kubrick's work as far back as *The Killing*, while also appearing in the uncensored version of *Spartacus*, *A Clockwork Orange*, *The Shining*, and *Eyes Wide Shut*). Robert Kolker points out that the two soldiers, "despite demonstrating some stereotypes of movie homosexuals, express a devotion to each other unlike any of the straight characters in the film" (Kolker 158), which adds another level of irony to the subsequent sequence with Lischen, the emotion of which at its close is undermined by The Narrator, as we have seen.

It is on the path to Lischen's that "Barry felt once more he was in his proper sphere and determined to never again fall from the rank of a gentleman," in the words of The Narrator, and one wonders if he might not have had better luck had he not stopped for the "romantic" sojourn. It is a pattern in Barry's life that his inability to control his emotions and passions lays waste to his plans (putting his ultimate choice to spare Bullingdon into relief). Thus fate has other things in store for Redmond Barry; just as The Narrator's talk of pickpockets and poachers led to Barry's deceitful departure from the British army, here his commentary that the Prussian army was filled by "scores of recruiters who would hesitate at no crime, including kidnapping, to keep supplied those brilliant regiments" – shown over images of callow youths in the dress of the Prussian military – leads immediately into a sequence where Barry is essentially blackmailed into the Prussian service by Hardy Kruger's Captain Potzdorf.

"[H]e is not very bright," Kubrick allowed of Barry (Schickel 163), and that is clearly in evidence in his failed attempt to deceive Potzdorf, brazenly claiming that his uncle "O'Grady" is an ambassador in Berlin, and failing even to properly recall the name of the general to whom he is meant to be delivering his "urgent dispatches," instead naming one who has been "dead these ten months." The Prussian service, however, allows him to expand his skills of prevarication. The Narrator quickly informs us that Barry has run into the worst company, and becomes "advanced in most every kind of misconduct," words spoken over rather calm images of Barry performing innocuous military tasks. Many writers have expressed some confusion as to why we hear about this, but don't actually see it; Kolker echoed a sentiment that "[perhaps] ... Kubrick was so sensitive to the criticism of violence in *A Clockwork Orange* that he did not film sequences that would bear out the narrator's words" (Kolker 158-159), but it seems evident that the reason is that Kubrick did not see the need for the visual and the vocal to provide redundant information. While the following sequence, wherein Barry risks his life to save Captain Potzdorf, might seem to belie The Narrator's accusations, they are essentially repeated by a commanding officer awarding Barry with a medal for his bravery, as he calls Barry "idle, dissolute, and unprincipled," predicting that "for all [his] talents and bravery, I am sure [he] will come to no good." Barry lies, implying that Potzdorf is the first "kind friend and protector" he has enjoyed, and saying while the colonel might say he is "a ruined lad, and send me to the devil," he "would go to the devil to serve the regiment." This speech introduces a march from Mozart's *Idomeneo* which continues to serve as a theme for Barry's scripted sycophancy.

Perhaps this reading is harsh, and Barry truly does feel some loyalty and affection for Potzdorf. But we see this neither dramatized nor uttered by other characters, as we so often do in regards to Barry's emotions. There can be no doubt as to Barry's affection for Grogan, as he personally carries Grogan's body away from the battlefield, kisses him, and weeps heavily when he passes away (his carriage of the fallen officer proving futile, unlike with Potzdorf). All we have to represent his devotion to his Prussian superior are things he says when it would serve him best to say them. There was still a hint of Barry's innocence even in his encounter with Lischen — after lying to her about being Fakenham when they first meet, upon their farewell she calls him by his real name — this sincerity feels washed away and empty. Potzdorf seems utterly fooled, and invests a confidence in Barry that will lead to Barry's reunion with a countryman and his immediate betrayal of his so-called "kind friend and protector."

CHAPTER FIVE
A SPY IN THE HOUSE OF CARDS

DIRECTING A SCENE IS largely about point of view. Kubrick did not pre-plan the shooting of his scenes in terms of coverage and composition; he felt that "[t]he first thing to do is rehearse the scene until something happens that is worth putting on film – only then should you worry about *how* to film it. The *what* must always precede the *how*" (Ciment 152). Kubrick then trusted his own camera skill to find the most interesting and effective shots. "The visual part of film-making has always come easiest to me, and that is why I am careful to subordinate it to the story and the performances," he told Ciment (177). (His photojournalistic experience as a youth with *Look* magazine may well have been his model here.) Even so, according to Ryan O'Neal, "[t]he toughest part of Stanley's day was finding the right first shot. Once he did that, other shots fell into place" (Schickel 166).

Kubrick's stated view of giving primacy to the *what* rather than the *how* may sound surprising coming from a director so renowned for his iconic imagery, as might also his oft-repeated contrast between Chaplin and Eisenstein (e.g., to Joseph Gelmis): "anyone seriously interested in comparative film techniques should study the differences in approach of [...] Eisenstein and Chaplin. Eisenstein is all form and no content, whereas Chaplin is content and no form" (Gelmis 316). Between these two extremes, Kubrick favored Chaplin, telling Philip Strick and Penelope Houston that Chaplin's "films will probably last longer than anyone else's," while decrying the silliness of Eisenstein's content (Strick and Houston 135). But, of course, the punchline follows: "Obviously, if you can combine style and content, you have the best of all possible films" (ibid.).

Kubrick tended not to speak too heavily toward his intentions, disliking "conceptualizing questions" (Cahill 370), so we have essentially no record of his thought process when putting together a scene visually. But, as we have seen, there are evident strategies that come into play throughout *Barry Lyndon* – the left-to-right vs. right-to-left movement, the prevalence of scene-setting zoom-outs, the use of zoom-in to accompany The Narrator's description of Barry's thoughts, and so forth. Even with our lacking confirmation from the director as to his intentions, these patterns are sufficiently prevalent that it seems safe to assume they are by design – but, even on the slight chance that they were not, their coherence has an impact on the viewer regardless.

The meeting of Barry and the Chevalier de Baliberi, after Barry has been sent to spy on the Chevalier, a suspected Irish spy himself, only to break down and reveal himself to the elder man, provides a simple yet telling demonstration of the thought put into the film's visual design and cutting. The scene opens in longshot (Setup 1); the Chevalier sits at a desk in the bottom right of the screen, his back to us. Barry enters, distant, in the center of the frame. Mozart's march plays until Barry's walk toward the desk is complete, where he stops and bows.

The Chevalier and Barry speak pleasantries in German; the following shot is a centered medium shot of the seated Chevalier as he delivers an untranslated line (Setup 2). We return to Setup 1 as Barry hands the Chevalier a reference letter, and again to Setup 2 as the Chevalier unfolds it to read it. The Chevalier reads Barry's fake name (one of four names by which Barry goes over the course of the film – identity is an overlooked recurring theme in Kubrick's work; think also of Jack Torrance always being "the caretaker", the nicknames immediately assigned to sever Marine trainees from their past selves in *Full Metal Jacket*, and Dr. Bill Harford's comically constant references to his medical ID over the course of his frustrating evening – and Barry's primal driving force is to become someone he is not), and Barry's response is shot in close-up (Setup 3). We return to Setup 2 as the Chevalier refers to the letter, and then an over-the-shoulder medium shot similar to but slightly more intimate than Setup 1, shot with a longer lens, again favoring Barry with the back of the Chevalier's head and shoulders in the bottom right of the frame (Setup 4). Setup 2 returns as the Chevalier takes in a response from Barry and returns to the letter. The Narrator chimes in here, beginning a passage that tells us that Barry is about to do something "imprudent," and we cut back to Barry's close-up of Setup 3 as he continues – again, we see a relatively impassive Barry as another speaker (here, The Narrator), speaks to his emotions. But Barry does start to emote as The Narrator speaks of "the burst of feeling" that is imminent, and we cut back to Setup 2 as the Chevalier completes his reading of the letter and looks up.

Setup 3 of an emotional Barry, Setup 2 of a concerned Chevalier, Setup 3 of Barry beginning to speak in English, and back to Setup 2 of the Chevalier as he hears Barry's confession. Setup 3 of Barry returns as he continues his confession and at last breaks into tears. The Chevalier's reaction is in Setup 2 –

– but then, as he gets up to comfort Barry, we cut to a brand new shot, a medium shot from *behind* Barry, portraying the full-length body of both men as the Chevalier circles his desk to embrace the weeping protagonist. This brand new shot, Setup 5, appears *only* when the circumstances of the men's acquaintance has completely changed, and has been reversed from the circumstances by which they were introduced into each other's company.

We do not know if, either on set or in the cutting room, Kubrick thought explicitly of the notion of "point of view" when constructing the images of this scene. We don't even know what the "first shot" was that he may have grappled with before identifying what coverage he needed. But we see the longest shot when they characters are the most remote, resort to close-ups when emotional responses need to be conveyed, and then see a more intimate version of the initial longer shot as they begin to know each other. And the scene concludes on a new shot, the signpost of a new relationship in Barry's life, and arguably the most impactful "replacement father" he will find.

Detractors and supporters alike point to Kubrick's apparent "objectivity" in his directorial style, frequently accounted for by his use of wide lenses, which distort character's faces and exaggerate the distances between them in frames; a compositional strategy that often seeks to situate characters as smaller pieces within a larger construct or landscape, thus minimizing their visual importance in relation to their surroundings (leading to, in the eyes of some, a minimization of their agency at the expense of larger, more immutable forces – which of course is often the point); and a relative lack of over-the-shoulder shots, a common aspect of film grammar which situates conversing characters in the same frame throughout a conversation. Kubrick's frequent use of singles or master shots in dialogue scenes, rather than the more conventional over-the-shoulder arrangement, isolates his characters in the frame, thus further isolating them from each other from a dramaturgical standpoint. Kubrick does, in this film, employ over-the-shoulder shots during scenes of tenderness, such as with Grogan and Lischen, but one benefit of a pattern is that the breaking of it carries greater significance. Here, in the scene with the Chevalier, the single shots disappear at the moment Barry and the Chevalier come together and ally, and the visual direction of the scene – and the dramatic trajectory of their lives – changes. Perhaps this is "objective" and "unfeeling", though a more fruitful approach would be to observe that there *is* feeling here (Martin Scorsese, after all, in an interview with Charlier Rose after Kubrick's passing, labeled *Barry Lyndon* "profoundly emotional"), and that this feeling is conveyed in the voiceover, the dialogue, and in the formal aspects of the scene's construction. It is feeling that must be earned, for the characters and for the viewer: "Obviously, if you can combine style and content, you have the best of all possible films."

The scene opens with Barry coming to the Chevalier, and closes with the Chevalier coming to Barry, and now Barry, already trained in misconduct, is taken under the wing of a more schooled and elegant master.

Despite claiming his is an "honorable profession" in which he gambles against "gentlemen of all the courts of Europe," the Chevalier is a cheat, and immediately enlists Barry in his schemes. A local prince can sense something is amiss, but cannot identify the source, when the Chevalier takes him for large sums one evening at the gaming table (the prince even hands Barry a tip on his way out), and, very quickly, the seeds for Barry's departure from the Prussian service are sewn. At this juncture, the film takes on a quicker pace, no longer setting up scenes with languorous zooms or pans, simply cutting from one image to another, most vignettes being presented in one brief shot. The Narrator also stays out of it, for the moment – but then he returns to *lie* to the audience, remarking that Barry-disguised-as-Chevalier is the Chevalier himself. The audience is not fooled for more than a split second, so perhaps The Narrator's deception is harmless, but one does wonder if there are other, less obvious deceptions The Narrator foists upon us.

Nonetheless, Barry and the Chevalier move on to continue their own deceptions at the various courts of Europe, and Barry once again resolves "hence forward and forever to live the life of a gentleman." Naturally, Barry's and the Chevalier's dealings with "gentlemen" are largely and literally underhanded; we spy the Chevalier dipping his hand below the table to pull a needed card out of his sleeve, thus defeating a nobleman named Lord Ludd (Steven Berkoff). We don't see Ludd accuse the men of cheating, but his refusal to pay leads him into a fencing duel with Barry, with Barry's victory sealing the Lord's obligation to cure his debt. Barry's life thus hinges on duels again, though, in this case, non-lethal ones; the gentleman class plays at duels much in the same way they play at cards. Much like Barry's military life, the aristocratic world in which he now finds himself is dependent upon a sense of order, one Barry eventually tries and fails to upset. The rustic countrysides of the film's opening sequences give way to enclosed spaces (the first two duels were set in expansive landscapes, while the sword duel with Lord Ludd is in an enclosed garden, and the climactic duel with Bullingdon in a dilapidated barn) and simple clothes give way to expensive gowns, and unadorned men's faces are replaced by men wearing makeup and marks to hide their blemishes. The candle-lit scenes, which initially conveyed intimate duos of Barry-Grogan and Barry-Lischen, now become more populated, as scores of candles illuminate the shady dealings of the gaming table.

Despite the "adventure" of this life, it is not all that Barry hopes for. The Narrator tells us early on that Barry was "destined to live the life of a wanderer," and he answers his own prophecy by describing Barry and the Chevalier's existence as "a wandering and disconnected life," further declaring that the pair don't have much in the way of material wealth. In the narrative pattern established by the film, where The Narrator's assertions of Barry's needs conjure imminent solutions, here this remark serves as the introduction into Barry's life and the story Lady Lyndon. Though The Narrator informs us that Barry has lost all romantic notions of love, thus seeing a potential marriage to Lady Lyndon as being a solely commercial transaction, the music and action play out in a lushly romantic manner, again exemplifying the use of The Narrator to give voice to sentiments that Barry cannot utter himself as he undertakes a seduction. To begin with, a new musical love theme is introduced in Schubert's Trio No. 3 in E Flat. Strictly speaking, the piece is anachronistic to the setting (written in 1827, thirty-eight years after *Barry Lyndon*'s final scene), something for which Kubrick was nearly apologetic in discussing it with Michel Ciment, as he had originally planned to use only music that was period-appropriate, further making the odd claim that "there are no tragic love-themes in eighteenth-century music" (Ciment 174) (this is, perhaps, an opportune time to mention that these published interviews were edited by Kubrick, both after recording and between the French and English publications; the actual audio of this passage is excerpted in a Criterion Collection home media feature on the making of the film, informing us that Kubrick extemporaneously had said "there is nothing even remotely that can pass for a love theme that has the sort of tragic, passionate feeling that this Schubert trio had"). To state just one example from more recent cinema, Terrence Malick's use of Mozart's Piano Concerto No. 23 in *The New World* is highly reminiscent of Kubrick's use of the Schubert Trio here, and given the amount of period-specific Mozart and Haydn Kubrick considered for the film (Castle KA 436), it seems unlikely that he didn't come across the piece while making his selections. The simplest explanation is that the Schubert is simply the piece that best exemplified, in the director's words, "just the right restrained balance between the tragic and the romantic" (Ciment 174) he found suitable for the sequence. What's more, as a twentieth-century film made from a nineteenth-century novel about the eighteenth-century, narrated by a figure who clearly post-dates the film's events, it seems only natural that the music need not obey any temporal rules: any zoom back from the eighteenth century to the twentieth must pass through the nineteenth. (Schubert music also marks the intermission breaks and certain sequences in the film's second half, discussed below.)

The contrast between the Schubert and the "Women of Ireland" love theme is illuminating. Unlike the lyrical nature and more free-flowing rhythm of the earlier folk melody, Schubert's Trio almost takes on the character of a march, with its insistent rhythms anchoring the main theme.

A more regimented piece, it fits comfortably into the structured world of the aristocracy, another complete departure from the rustic and traditional sound of the Irish countryside, just as we've seen with the sets and costumes; the respective romantic themes each represent their setting.

Schubert's piece is introduced over an establishing shot of a mountain castle, then proceeds through The Narrator's revelation of Barry's designs on marriage, as well as our first sighting of Lady Lyndon, along with her elderly, wheelchair-bound husband, their child son, and her chaplain (Michael Klein points out that the first zoom into Lady Lyndon is matched with a shift in the piece from a minor to a major key [Klein]). But the bulk of the music accompanies a lengthy, wordless seduction scene as Barry and Lady Lyndon spy each other from across a gaming table. The bank of candles both flatters Marisa Berenson and gives her a ghostly pallor, matched by the pale makeup worn by Barry, casting a dreamlike mood over their encounter. As the Reverend Runt looks on disapprovingly, Barry and the Lady cannot stop exchanging glances; he slides some chips over to her so she can engage in the game. Cuts sync with the music, and Lady Lyndon excuses herself to get a "bit of air." She waits on a balcony, glowing white in the moonlight, and Barry follows, slowly walking (left to right, of course) up behind her, precipitating their first kiss. (Again, Kubrick raids *Napoleon* here, adapting elements from two different scenes: he depicts Napoleon as first seeing Josephine at a gaming table [Kubrick 20], and the first kiss between Josephine and her extramarital paramour Hippolyte Charles is staged in an exterior garden by moonlight in a similar fashion to the balcony scene here [43].)

"It's very romantic," Kubrick told Ciment, "but at the same time, I think it suggests the empty attraction they have for each other that is to disappear as quickly as it arose" (Ciment 174). Romance in Kubrick, to the extent it even exists, is hardly ever motivated by a congruence of personalities; it is telling that Kubrick had initially scripted the courtship of Lady Lyndon in lengthy dialogue sequences, only to cut it down to its barest visual essentials. While Raphael's report implies that Kubrick perhaps cut the dialogue out of concern for Berenson's ability to perform it, the final sequence is far more evocative of Kubrick's typical styles, themes, and, as reflected in the above comment to Ciment, the true nature of the characters and their relationship. The meeting and falling-in-love between Spartacus and Varinia is actually depicted in a similar manner to this Barry-Lady Lyndon sequence, as it comprises silent looks and romantic music. (One might even argue that this leads *that* particular romance to feel as empty as the one between Barry and the Lady, though this becomes far more problematic in that film as we are asked to take the romance seriously.) Kubrick attempted a more traditional and happy romance in his early film noir, *Killer's Kiss*, but the desperate love that grows out of Humbert Humbert's illicit attraction to the underage Lolita feels more in the spirit of Kubrick's work, as does the distrust and infidelity of the marriage between the Elisha Cook, Jr. and Marie Windsor characters in *The Killing* (whereas the loyal love interest for Sterling Hayden's Johnny is essentially a non-entity, with little screentime and negligible plot significance). Romance is completely absent from the "science fiction trilogy" of *Dr. Strangelove, 2001,* and *A Clockwork Orange,* and it's difficult to imagine Jack Torrance courting Wendy. It was not until Kubrick finally realized *Eyes Wide Shut* that we see a believable married couple that at least *seems* happy on its surface (though Barry and Lady Lyndon must pretend to be to comport with the rules of society), though of course the entirety of that film is about undercutting that surface image.

"To make a long story short," The Narrator says, as though to hint to us that he has a sense of humor, "her ladyship was in love." Barry, unusually for him, wears red, and a red sail appears behind the happy couple as they take a relaxed boat ride around a lake; the whole world luxuriates in the splendor of love. As with the preparations for Barry's and the Chevalier's departure from Prussia, the brief glimpses we are given of this affair forego any use of the zoom, simply cutting from one image to another. The slow pan does make an appearance, however, as Barry and Lady Lyndon stride on an elevated walkway over a beautiful garden and river: Barry at last finds himself in a position where he can gaze down on the state of others. It is only from such heights that man can fall.

CHAPTER SIX
ALL THE BEST PEOPLE

THE REVEREND RUNT'S WEDDING sermon is an accusation. He glares at Barry as he states that "marriage should not be entered into unadvisedly," and that marriage should not serve to "satisfy men's carnal lusts." His visage warms as he turns to Lady Lyndon to say that marriage should be entered into "reverently, discretely, advisedly, soberly and in the fear of God." The camera follows suit, cutting to Lord Bullingdon as Runt speaks of marriage being "ordained, first, [...] for the procreation of children," and then to a close-up of Barry when he says, "secondly, it was ordained as a remedy against sin and to avoid fornication."

The title card opening the film's second part advises us as to Barry's eventual doom, and the film wastes no time in undercutting any joy we might have anticipated from the Barry-Lyndon union. Immediately after the wedding we see the right-to-left movement of their carriage and the film introduces the sad, mournful musical theme of Barry's decline, the third movement of Vivaldi's Cello Concerto in E minor; Barry's social rise is thus imbued with a sense of loss and tragedy, even before the promised "misfortunes" befall him. Not that he does anything to gain sympathy, blowing unwanted smoke in his wife's face as they ride home from their nuptials. Lord Bullingdon, in the meantime, correctly appraises Barry's opportunistic character while in conversation with Runt in their own carriage (though when he refers to Barry as a "common opportunist", it is difficult to tell which word causes him more grief).

Runt says the first purpose of marriage is the procreation of children, and thus we cut from the post-wedding conversations to a zoom-out of Barry and Lady Lyndon lying with their newborn child, Bryan. However, the second purpose − "a remedy against sin and to avoid fornication" − is revealed to carry no weight with Barry, as we cut to a zoom-out of Barry kissing two topless women in an apparent brothel or club. And so the following shot is a zoom-out of a forlorn Lady Lyndon lying silently with Bullingdon with the infant Bryan close at hand. Three consecutive shots, using the same zoom technique, tell a quick and efficient story of the rapid deterioration of a marriage that had little beyond circumstance to recommend it in the first place; an effective shorthanding reminiscent of the famed montage in *Citizen Kane* that ends with Kane and his wife sitting distant from each other at their dining table.

"Lady Lyndon was soon destined to occupy a place in Barry's life not very much more important than the elegant carpets and pictures which would form the pleasant background of his existence," asserts The Narrator, and shots such as these with Bullingdon and Bryan depict her as embodying the picture-like existence which Barry has assigned her. Some critics of the film found it, in the words of Pauline Kael, "a three-hour slide show for art history majors" (Kael 49), replete with the "museum-tour guide machine" of The Narrator (50), but here we see a thematic reason that so many of the compositions take on a painterly mien. In fact, Kubrick relied heavily upon period art so as to gain knowledge of period detail, and would utilize poses and compositions from specific paintings so as to create a seeming documentary of pre-Napoleonic Europe. Ryan O'Neal reported that once when Kubrick "was really stymied [about a shot], [h]e found a painting ... and posed Marisa and me exactly as if we were in that painting" (Schickel 166). One scholar "claims to have identified 271 paintings woven into the fabric" of the film (Fischer 173); these are not necessarily direct citations or re-creations, but borrowings: the posture of a gentleman passed out in a chair in Hogarth's *Marriage Ala Mode: The Morning After*, for instance, finds reprise in the unconscious Barry both after Bryan's death and when he is found and challenged to a duel by Bullingdon (Wickre 182-183). Other small details of the film certainly feel as though they were plucked from paintings – think of the short procession of children skipping near the end of the military parade that re-introduces Barry to Grogan. Jan Harlan, Kubrick's brother-in-law and eventual executive producer, pointed out that the director learned from paintings how households would place tables near windows to maximize exposure to light (Pulver). Period art served as Kubrick's window into the nonverbal behaviors of the time.

Citations of paintings were nothing new in Kubrick's work; the chateau that serves as the military command center in *Paths of Glory* is decorated with elegant "carpets and pictures" (providing a contrast between officer life and those of the soldiers in the muddy trenches), and Humbert Humbert shoots Clare Quilty dead through a Gainsboroughesque portrait. Famously, the waiting room beyond *2001*'s infinite takes on a Victorian character, and the final shot of *A Clockwork Orange* might presage *Barry Lyndon* by depicting a sexual fantasy of Alex's in which his romp is applauded by a Victorian audience. In fact, it actually seems that the *Victorian* was the period most appealing to Kubrick on an aesthetic level. *Barry Lyndon* (and *Strangelove*) production designer Ken Adam, who gained an Oscar and a nervous breakdown for his efforts, reported that he had to go to great lengths to prove to Kubrick that some of his initial choices of interiors and wallpapers were unsuitable for the film as they originated in the Victorian rather than the more period-appropriate "formal, stark, eighteenth-century interiors" (LoBrutto 381).

While this "formal, stark" setting and the compositional tendency to emulate paintings and poses, combined with the inability of actors to move for focus-based reasons in the candlelit sequences, threaten to give the film a static feel, a sense of motion is enhanced by the frequent zooms, pans, and the juxtaposition of successive shots, which is often informed by the voiceover narration. While, as discussed above, this constructivist approach to sequence design might have its roots in Kubrick's early reading of Pudovkin, this film's manner of constructing scenes (as opposed to constructing sequences) is diametrically opposed to Pudovkin's ideal of "eliminating moments that are unnecessary or immaterial to the action" (Aumont 11). From the shot of Lady Lyndon and her children we get another slow pan, establishing a scene where she, Bullingdon, and Runt play a piece of chamber music. Unlike the previous three mini-scenes, this scene does include cuts, as we cut from a melancholy Lady Lyndon's gaze as she plays the harpsichord to the object of same, Bullingdon at his cello. This further foregrounds the bond between Lady Lyndon and her eldest son, and this very same trio is the focus of the beginning of the following scene, when, walking through a garden, they spy Barry kissing one of his maids as they stand next to Bryan's stroller. Bullingdon, foreshadowing his desire to protect his mother, takes her hand in comfort. The cutting pattern similarly foreshadows the film's climactic conflict, as the first reaction shot we see amongst the three is that of *Bullingdon*, cutting back to their semi-point-of-view of Barry and the maid before cutting to Lady Lyndon's first close-up of the scene. But now The Narrator points out that she "finds rivals even among her maids," and, in response, the following image is that of Lady Lyndon playing cards with her maids – a far more benign "rivalry" than she might have with those who might seduce (or let themselves be seduced by) her husband, but an immediate proof of The Narrator's claims is offered – it appears that all women are her rivals to one degree or another (this network of rivalry will be expanded once Barry's mother exerts her own influence on her son and the estate).

The failure of marriage to govern Barry's lusts exhibits a common theme of Kubrick's, playing off his skepticism about human institutions generally and of marriage specifically. Institutions are made by man, and thus subject to the same corruptions and limitations as their creators. Hence the elaborate security structures of *Dr. Strangelove* can lead to apocalypse when foiled by a determined madman. One of the underlying thematic premises of *A Clockwork Orange*, made more explicit in the novel but still extant in the adaptation, is that any change for good must be motivated from within an individual, and that outside influences such as school, family, the justice system, science, and religion cannot impose betterment on the unwilling. We see this application to marriage in Humbert Humbert's dishonest marriage to Charlotte Haze, all a gambit for him to increase his proximity to her daughter. Jack Torrance has a roving eye, casting glances at young female employees leaving The Overlook and facing the temptation of a nude seductress in Room 237. *Eyes Wide Shut*, of course, makes the inability of marriage to limit either men's or women's "carnal lusts" or to provide a "remedy against sin and to avoid fornication" its central subject, narratively and thematically. "Don't you think one of the charms of marriage," says one character attempting to seduce Alice Harford, "is that it makes deception a necessity for both parties?" (*Eyes Wide Shut* also finally satisfied what appeared to be a longstanding desire in Kubrick's career to film an orgy, perhaps the basis upon which we are shown the two topless whores here. He pressed Felix Markham on the orgies Josephine might have taken part in as organized by Napoleon contemporary Paul Barras, and must have been disappointed when the historian said "I don't think it was exactly orgiastic" [Ellis 116]. Kubrick converted this impulse to a live sex show witnessed by a high-class crowd that included both Napoleon and Josephine in his screenplay [Kubrick 23-24]. The director also contemplated making sex more of a driving force in *The Shining* [McAvoy 548-549], and considered turning the ghostly 1920s party Jack stumbles upon into an orgy [549-550]. Naturally, these might also have been attempts to infuse these other projects with the specter of Schnitzler at a time before Kubrick knew he would eventually adapt it.)

It seems that the scene that O'Neal referred to where Kubrick posed his two leads according to a painting might well be the subsequent scene wherein Barry, the next morning, visits Lady Lyndon at her bath and apologizes; a painting of a man kneeling in front of a woman rests on the wall behind them. The painting practically mocks Barry by displaying how much of his comportment is a pose designed to fit into his surroundings; even before Barry's entrance in the scene, one of Lady Lyndon's attendants is reading to her a poem in French that speaks to the reuniting of lovers (Ciment 110). Ciment finds this "[a] moment of stability" in the relationship (113), seemingly taking Barry's apology at face value. But isn't the poem yet another representation of a role Barry is attempting to play? Be it gentleman or obsequious husband, whether inspired by poem or painting, all are parts played insincerely by Barry Lyndon. "When we try to deceive we are convincing as we can be, aren't we?"

Nonetheless, Lady Lyndon appears to accept his apology with a kiss, but the next scene presents an unforgiving Bullingdon, chiding his mother for the marriage and *refusing* to kiss his stepfather goodbye. Barry responds, as discussed above, with the only disciplinary technique at his disposal, taking a rod to the child's backside as he learned from the gauntlet of the Prussian army. Bullingdon leaves the room chastised, but the next shot jumps nearly eight years, as a now teenage Bullingdon has a more tender physical moment, sitting at his mother's feet and holding her hand as she, Barry, Barry's mother, and countless others watch a magic show celebrating Bryan's eighth birthday, the last he will ever have. (Bryan is also shown enjoying a ride in a lamb-drawn carriage – another *Napoleon* lift [Kubrick 125].)

On-screen, at least, Ryan O'Neal is very good with children. The most famous case is his performance alongside his tyke daughter Tatum in Peter Bogdanovich's *Paper Moon*, for which she won an Oscar. There is a generosity that allows children to be their best, and that extends to Barry's relationship with Bryan, played by David Morley, here. Dominic Savage, who plays the young Bullingdon (and grew up to be a director himself), and Morley are the first two child actors to have prominent roles in a Kubrick film (Sue Lyon being a teenager in *Lolita*); Danny Lloyd would follow in *The Shining*. Neither Lloyd nor Morley pursued acting, making only rare appearances in other films before pursuing other careers. It would appear that Kubrick preferred not to work with professional child actors, perhaps finding the less-trained to be the more-natural. The relationship between Barry and Bryan is the true emotional core of the film, and while the child isn't asked to carry heavy weight, he delivers on all he is asked.

Of course, like all other aspects of Barry's life, Bryan is doomed, though The Narrator waits to tell us this. We do get a bit foreshadowing when Barry tells Bryan a tall tale about his war days, wherein he mentions that a prince "burst into tears" – the next time he tells the story, it will Barry himself who so bursts. After the war story, Bryan asks his father if he will tell him another story the next day, and then if he will play cards with him the next day. From war, to telling stories, to playing cards, the activities Bryan wants to enjoy with his father follow the trajectory of Barry's life before meeting his mother.

These opening passages of the film's second half establish the main alliances that provide the foundation for the conflicts that follow: Barry's estrangement from Lady Lyndon, Lord Bullingdon's outright contempt for Barry that is answered with violence, and Barry's devotion to his own son. Barry's mother fills a narrational role by bluntly setting forth to her son the stakes at hand; the fortune he enjoys is only at the mercy of an ambivalent wife and a nemesis stepson, and any dissolution of the marriage could prove ruinous for Barry and his beloved son (not to mention his mother). It is for that reason that she urges him to pursue a title and peerage, the quest that will seal his decline.

Barry's campaign begins with Barry seeking the counsel of Lord Hallon (the government minister played by Anthony Sharp), who in turn introduces him to Lord Wendover. Wendover brags to Barry that those he takes on are "the best people." This phrase, which is not in Thackeray's novel, is a recurring motif in Kubrick's films. Humbert Humbert says that "all the best people shave twice a day" and The Overlook's manager tells his new caretaker and family that "all the best people" have stayed at the hotel (in all three cases, the phrase has no basis in the source). The expression drips with condescension and is presented with irony. Wendover expounds; he does not mean that "the best people" are the richest or most virtuous or the best-born, but "people about whom there is no question" (this definition does come from the pages of Thackeray, but not from the pages of *Barry Lyndon* – they originate in *Vanity Fair* as a description of "the best" who are received into the company Becky Sharp [Thackeray VF]; Kubrick told Ciment he had considered adapting *Vanity Fair* before rejecting it due to concerns of length – and intriguingly and prophetically pointed out that longform television served as a solution to this eternal problem of adaptation [Ciment 167]). Wendover's implication is that merit is not a factor; success in society is derived from connections and not from any intrinsic worth, achievement, or even grace. Such connections as Barry has prove tenuous, and are sundered when he violates the veneer of decency by assaulting Bullingdon.

Kubrick links Barry's love for his son to his desire for a peerage by using the same Schubert German Dance to accompany Bryan's birthday party as he does to underscore a montage of Barry, under the supervision of Hallon and Wendover, beginning his quest, a quest defined entirely by extravagant spending. Again, this is communicated efficiently, with three consecutive one-shot scenes: one of a lavish dinner party (reminiscent of one in *The Scarlet Empress,* a film Ciment sees as similar to *Barry Lyndon* in its "use of music and commentary" and its "direction of actors and [...] irony" [66]), one of Barry engaging in profligate spending on a painting by an obscure artist (in likely reference to *A Clockwork Orange*'s Ludovico Technique, the painting is *The Adoration of the Magi* by Ludovico Cardi, also known as Cigoli), and one of Barry in audience with King George III, who is informed that Barry has raised a battalion to fight the American rebels (certainly a costly venture). The Narrator speaks to the escalating costs and we see the silent and stressed countenance of the estate accountant.

If we associate Barry's "blind partiality" (as The Narrator puts it) to his son with his financially ruinous social aspirations, it also pairs with the cause of his ultimate rift with Bullingdon. When Bullingdon takes it upon himself to spank Bryan over a silly schoolroom conflict (like stepfather, like stepson), Barry intervenes and once again canes the now-teenage lord. Bullingdon announces that he "will accept no further chastisement" from the man he insists on addressing as "Mr. Redmond Barry", going so far as to threaten Barry's life should he strike him again. But Bullingdon does not wait to exact his revenge.

The scene in which Bullingdon interrupts a concert and Barry strikes him is an elegant representation of how Kubrick's strategies of withholding and releasing information throughout the film create suspense and build and release narrative tension. The scene begins with a shot of a chamber orchestra, in the music room in which we previously saw Lady Lyndon play with Runt and the younger Bullingdon. A slow pan reveals Lady Lyndon once again at the harpsichord, and the Reverend Runt again on the flute. Bullingdon, however, is nowhere in sight, and if we recall the previous scene, we might wonder where he is. The pan continues to reveal a large-ish crowd, comprising many of the noblemen and benefactors we have come to recognize as being party to Barry's peerage pursuit, notably Lords Hallon and Wendover. Barry himself sits in the front row. Again, Bullingdon is absent. We cut to a closed door at the back of the room, behind the audience. Centered in the frame, the closed door invites us to speculate on its importance, and within moments Bullingdon enters, guiding by the hand Bryan, wearing Bullingdon's shoes, oversized for the youth and clanking on the floor as Bullingdon leads him toward the performance. A tracking shot precedes them, and the audience around them reacts, generally with some amusement at the adorable young child. But Barry's reaction is unseen to us – we know him to be at the front of the room, so as Bullingdon and Barry slowly proceed in that direction, creating ever more distraction from the concert, we are made to speculate on Barry's reaction. When it is finally revealed, his anger (exemplified in the traditional "Kubrick stare") is palpable, as is Lady Lyndon's when she is at last shown. Each of these camera set-ups, each camera movement, and each cut are thoughtfully designed to raise and answer narrative questions in turn.

The concert interrupted, Bullingdon levels his accusations at Barry, decrying his "open infidelity" (we have actually not seen Barry act unfaithfully since the sequence with the maid, set nearly eight years prior to this one, so it is impossible for the audience to judge with certainty whether this is an old or evergreen complaint) and impugning his comparatively modest background. Lady Lyndon spurns Bullingdon, expressing her love for Bryan and implying that her heart has hardened in relation to her elder son. When she takes Bryan out of the room, Barry has had enough, and assaults Bullingdon from behind. It takes a large group of onlookers, comically slipping and sliding across the shiny floor, to restrain Barry. For it is Barry who has committed the most grievous sin in the eyes of society; Bullingdon is a Lord, and while his interruption of the musical performance betrays a lack of manners and might rightly infuriate Barry, Barry's resorting, once again, to violence as a form of conflict resolution (recall that the shaky handheld camera from the army boxing match is reprised here) is frowned upon; "frightful behavior" we can read on the lips of Lord Hallon. One simply does not strike a lord.

The mournful Vivaldi theme returns as Barry stands isolated on the grounds of Castle Hackton, alone and abandoned. We then cut to a restaurant, where Lord Wendover enters to eat alone. In a single shot, we pan with him and the host as he is seated (John Alcott reported that this was the most difficult shot of the entire film, given the challenges of maintaining consistent lighting through the large windows that provide the room's illumination [Alcott]). In another example of carefully released information, it is only now that we see that Barry is also a patron here, seated alone, in the composition's background. The one-shot scene continues as Barry approaches Wendover, inviting him to join him, and inviting him to dinner at his home at a future date. The elder noble politely but definitively rebuffs these advances; Barry has been expelled from the brotherhood of The Best People. So chastised, he returns to his table to eat alone.

Markham: "He wasn't one of them." Kubrick: "He must have felt this all the time."

CHAPTER SEVEN
ALL EQUAL NOW

DAVID BORDWELL, LARGELY IN reference to the international art cinema of the 1950s and 1960s, has identified a set of narrational techniques that might typify "art cinema":

- "the goal-bereft protagonist", contrasted with the "Hollywood protagonist" who "speeds toward the target", whereas the "art-film protagonist is presented as sliding passively from one situation to another";
- "the episodic format", where "scenes are built around chance encounters, and the entire film may consist of nothing more than a series of them";
- the "central boundary situation", in which the narrative's "causal chain leads up to an episode of the private individual's awareness of fundamental human issues," such that "the film's causal impetus often derives from the protagonist's recognition that he or she faces a crisis of existential significance", in contrast to "classical film focus[ing] the spectator's expectations on the ongoing causal chain by shaping the [...] dramatic duration around explicit deadlines";
- "spatiotemporal 'expressive' effects", such as flashbacks or flash-forwards, freeze-frames, and other such devices meant to place the viewer into the subjective experience of the film's characters; and
- "overt narrational 'commentary'", wherein "the viewer looks for those moments in which the narrational act interrupts the transmission of [story] information and highlights its own role," such as "an unusual angle, a stressed bit of cutting, a striking camera movement [...] or any other breakdown of objective realism which is not motivated as subjectivity" (Bordwell 206-211).

Bordwell finds that these "art cinema" tropes have "roots in an opposition to Hollywood nurtured within various national film industries of the silent era and sustained by concepts borrowed from modernism in theater and literature" (229). Several critics identify Kubrick as a modernist, with James Naremore pointing to the artistic milieu he "absorbed" in 1940s and 1950s New York (Naremore 29), and Robert Kolker flatly stating that Kubrick's films "are modernist explorations of a universe made frightful by our own bad choices" (Kolker 174). This is the sort of "conceptualization" Kubrick was wary of indulging in interviews, though modernism's typical clash between rational and irrational and its emphasis on the grotesque (also extensively explored by Naremore in relation to Kubrick [Naremore 24-41]) certainly echo in Kubrick's work.

We have seen Kubrick's admiration of the silent film tradition Bordwell identifies, and a good number of the filmmakers Kubrick identified as influential upon him or admired by him in his early years as a public figure come from the art film tradition described: Bergman, Fellini, de Sica, Truffaut, Antonioni, and, though American, Welles. Even in later years, films that tended to appeal to him were frequently what are commercially considered art films, and often European (e.g. *The Battle of Algiers*; *Closely Observed Trains*; Carlos Saura's *Peppermint Frappé*, *Cría Cuervos*, and *Blood Wedding*; Adrzej Wajda's *Danton* [Wrigley]; and Claudia Weill's proto-mumblecore American feature *Girl Friends*, which he compared "with the serious, intelligent, sensitive writing and filmmaking that you find in the best directors *in Europe* [emphasis mine]" [Foix 460]). In the meantime, he seemed to have little regard for the postmodern avant-garde, bluntly asserting in one 1980 interview that he hadn't "seen any good underground movies [...] any underground films that [he] thought were important or particularly interesting" (461).

The art cinema hallmarks identified by Bordwell are strong presences in most Kubrick films and in *Barry Lyndon* in particular:

- "the goal-bereft protagonist" "sliding passively from one situation to another" is a *mostly*-apt descriptor of protagonists in *2001*, *A Clockwork Orange* from Alex's arrest forward, *Barry Lyndon*, *Full Metal Jacket*, and the first half of *Eyes Wide Shut* (though, as we have seen, Barry does have the goal of being a gentleman, but that goal differs from the Hollywood norm by the lack of "deadlines" as discussed below);
- "the episodic format" is typical of the picaresque, and makes its presence known in such *Barry Lyndon* encounters as those with Captain Feeny, Barry's reunion with Captain Grogan, his spying of the gay courier, and his ill-fated meeting of Potzdorf;
- the "central boundary situation" focused on "a crisis of existential significance", rather than "dramatic duration around explicit deadlines" applies to nearly all Kubrick films beyond such ticking-clock narratives as *The Killing* and *Dr. Strangelove*, and comes to a metaphorical head

in *2001*'s Stargate sequence, and a more intimate one here when Barry is faced with a moral choice at the climax of his duel with Bullingdon;

- "spatiotemporal 'expressive' effects" are most present in *A Clockwork Orange*, a film "told" to us in words, pictures, and musical score by its protagonist/narrator, but also apparent in some of the ghostly visions experienced by Danny in *The Shining* – even so, *Barry Lyndon* contains one slow-motion flashback and also features a climactic freeze-frame; and

- "overt narrational 'commentary'" often exists in the form of voiceover or other "distancing structures" (so labeled by Kolker, who rightly rejects an equation of such effects as used by Kubrick and those as used by Brecht, the patron saint of "distancing effects" [Kolker 167-168]), and in *Barry Lyndon* is personified in the voice of The Narrator.

Despite these tendencies, it does not seem that Kubrick sought to identify himself as an art film director, and in fact the vast majority of his films were financed and released as mainstream releases by venerable and commercial Hollywood studios; the relationship he enjoyed with Warner Bros. for his last five films bordered on patronage. His arrangement was unique in film history, largely a product of timing and his hitting his artistic and commercial stride at a time when Hollywood studios were in a panic and unusually deferential to the power of a creative filmmaker. Michael Herr noted that Kubrick "had great respect for the box office, if not the greatest respect, and found something to admire in even the most vile movie once it passed a hundred million" (Herr). Brian Aldiss, whose short story "Super-Toys Last All Summer Long" was the basis of *A.I.*, said that when discussing the development of the film with Kubrick the director wanted to devise a film "that would gross as much as *Star Wars*, while enabling him to retain his reputation for social responsibility" (Aldiss). This defines the unique space of "blockbuster art films" that comprise Kubrick's filmography, artistically adventurous and serious-minded pictures made under large budgets, affording big stars when needed, and enjoying wide theatrical release backed up by prodigious ad campaigns. Ironically, Kubrick himself stated it was "very hard to make a film that is both dramatically appealing to a wide audience and contains the kind of truth and perception which you associate with great literature" (Foix 460) – yet this is exactly the project of nearly all of his films after his early apprentice genre work.

This collision of art film tendencies with blockbuster release may be another factor that contributed to the mixed reactions Kubrick's films would engender upon release, reputations which over time have grown into a more universal positive appraisal. Hollywood films are indeed centered around goal-centered protagonists who create their own fates through decisive and dramatic action; as such, the frequent apparently "passive" protagonists of Kubrick's films are out of place, though central characters at the mercy of "chance encounters" align thematically with Kubrick's depiction of individual humans (or even humanity itself, such as in *2001*) at the mercy of powerful, overwhelming outside forces – forces often driven by the human flaws that might have instituted such forces (such as in *Strangelove*). But Kubrick ultimately locates the fault for these malicious forces within humanity itself, describing man as "an ignoble savage [...] irrational, brutal, weak, silly, unable to be objective about anything where his own interests are involved ... and any attempt to create social institutions based on a false view of the nature of man is probably doomed to failure" (Kubrick NYT 418). The fault – and the chance for improvement ("However vast the darkness, we must supply our own light," Kubrick told Eric Nordern in promoting *2001* [Nordern 353]) – are both assigned to human nature: "I don't think man is what he is because of an imperfectly structured society, but rather that society is imperfectly structured because of the nature of man," he told Michel Ciment (Ciment 163).

So is Bryan's death a "chance encounter" with the "grim invincible enemy", or is it rooted in Barry's over-indulgence of his beloved son? It seems a bitter pill that Barry's love for Bryan, his most and perhaps only redeeming quality for the bulk of the film, should be the reason he loses the last thing left in his life following his being discarded by society. But, as we have seen, Barry's inability to control his passions often leads to his defeat. And Kubrick's project of combining art film aesthetics with commercial demands leads to one of the most daring uses of "overt narrational commentary" in his work: as the Handel sarabande returns (for the first time since the Quin duel), we see Barry teaching Bryan to fence (a playful duel of its own), and The Narrator speaks of Barry's aspirations for "the lad", and further shots of the happy family playing croquet are accompanied by The Narrator's revelation that Barry will die childless. What follows is the most openly emotional sequence in any Kubrick film, a tearjerking ten minutes where the director basically dares his audience not to cry by stating its result at its onset.

Of course, we do not know, on a first viewing, that this is the sequence that will prove The Narrator's statement, but Barry is already in a bad way. After his dismissal by Wendover, a dark and foggy establishing shot of

Castle Hackton, and a despondent Lady Lyndon and Barry signing checks as "all the bills came down on him all at once," we see Barry silently fishing with Bryan on a small boat – such boats have been symbols of joy heretofore, carrying Barry and Lady Lyndon during their courtship, and a smiling Lady Lyndon and Bryan while Barry's mother pressed him about the peerage, but the context here is one of defeat. We then cut to a medium shot of Barry and Bryan sitting in a large room, reviewing the boy's drawings – and then cut to a distant shot as the scene continues, as father and son are dwarfed by a huge painting on the wall above them, an enormous family portrait (Anthony Van Dyck's *Philip, the 4th Earl of Pembroke, and His Family* [Wickre 184] – itself a doomed family "on the verge of collapse [Nicolson]) that may suggest "the moral and cultural weight of family lineage" (Wickre 180), a lineage we are about to learn will be deprived of the Barrys of Barryville. What's more, while this is exactly the sort of shot that is usually a continuous zoom-out in the film, here we have an abrupt cut from the intimate shot to the distant one – a formalistic harbinger of the tragedy to come.

As has become the film's strategy when it is time for the pace to quicken, the zoom disappears for the balance of the sequence. Bryan lobbies his father for a full-grown horse as his ninth birthday gift; though Barry expresses caution, it is clear that he will acquiesce to the request, and soon enough we see him making the purchase and sending the horse off for training. Kubrick the chess player has all the pieces where he wants them, and now it is time to simply, efficiently, and poignantly execute the endgame.

The sarabande, which in this section of the film is a light, stringed rendition, casts a dark spell over the entire sequence, continuing from the moment of the fencing and through Bryan's request and Barry's purchase to a dinner where Bryan reveals that he has learned of it – and his mother makes him promise that he will not go see the horse in advance of his birthday and that he shall never ride it without his father accompanying him. Every small detail of the discussion contributes to building the drama: while Bryan embraces his father in thanks for the presumed gift, it takes Lady Lyndon two attempts to gain Bryan's attention as she lays down this command, one supported by Barry as almost an afterthought when he promising his son a "whipping" should he disobey. But Bryan is, in at least one way too many, his father's son, and his youthful impetuousness leads him fatally astray.

The sarabande fades out as the Reverend Runt interrupts Barry as he takes his morning shave to inform him that Bryan has snuck off in the early morning. Barry rushes to the farm where the horse is being trained – only to discover that a badly-wounded Bryan is already being attended to – and here we get the rare bit of cinematic pyrotechnics in the slow-motion flashback of his fall, unmotivated by subjectivity (if anything, it's the point of view of the farmhand who spied the incident and first got to the boy), but there to provide visual weight to the farmhand's verbal account. Barry dismounts his horse and barks orders as the handheld camera, the film's formal indicator of a loss of control, makes a brief return, and assures his son that he will not follow through on his promise of whipping him for his indiscretion.

The sarabande returns as we cut to Barry and Lady Lyndon attending to Bryan on his deathbed. Lady Lyndon is in near-hysterics, where Barry tries hopelessly to keep a straight face. Bryan is calmest of all, and urges his parents to end their quarreling so that they might all meet again in heaven (this request comes directly from Thackeray's novel.) He further asks his father to repeat the war story we saw him tell before, an outlandish story about seizing a castle and cutting off the heads of the enemy soldiers (and an invention of Kubrick's).

Richard Schickel recounts the following story:

> Once after days of effort, [O'Neal] finally managed to deliver exactly what Kubrick wanted in a difficult scene. [O'Neal:] "He found a way to walk past me, giving instructions to the crew – 'Let's move on to thirty-two, move those lights into the foreground,' and so on – but as he passed me, he grabbed my hand and squeezed it. It was the most beautiful and appreciated gesture of my life. It was the greatest moment of my career" (Schickel 170).

I have always wondered what scene he was referring to, but I'm hard-pressed to find a greater moment in O'Neal's on-screen career than that in which he attempts to re-tell the war story, but his voice cracks, and his sobs mount, and he buries his head in his hands, all as the closing phrase of the sarabande, still played in a gentle arrangement, comes to a resolution, only to immediately come back stronger in the full orchestral, timpani-driven force that we heard over the opening credits, matching the cut from the disconsolate Barry to Bryan's funeral procession, a one-shot zoom-out as the lamb-drawn carriage moves from right to left, the Reverend Runt's intonations about eternal life competing with Handel's Rosenman-filtered strings, Barry and Lady Lyndon and Barry's mother shedding tears of their own, and I think maybe it zooms back in as the carriage and procession passes or maybe it all just gets really close to the camera, but to tell you for sure I'd have to watch the scene with dry eyes.

CHAPTER EIGHT
LIBERTY, EQUALITY, FRATERNITY

"DID YOU EVER SEE a worse performance than Vivien Leigh in *Gone with the Wind*?" Frederic Raphael quotes Kubrick as saying. "You know something? It's a really terrible movie" (Raphael 167).

Raphael posits this in the context of declaring that Kubrick's "sacred cows were all masculine" (ibid.) – as though distaste for either Leigh's performance or the film as a whole is gender-dependent. What seems more likely is that, beyond simply disliking the lead performance, Kubrick felt that *Gone with the Wind* failed *as a historical film*. In speaking to Philip Strick and Penelope Houston about his plans for *Napoleon*, Kubrick offered that he was starting "from the premise that there has never been a great historical film, and I say that with apologies and respect to those who have made historical films, including myself" (Strick and Houston 138). This did not necessarily mean that there had been no good films set in the past; he acknowledged in the same interview, for instance, that Abel Gance's *Napoleon* was "a masterpiece of cinematic invention and it brought cinematic innovations whenever someone is bold enough to try them again" (ibid.) (though he also told Joseph Gelmis that "as far as story and performance goes it's a very crude picture" [Gelmis 298]). The problem with historical films is that they failed as *history*, or at least *dramatic history*: "I don't think anyone has ever successfully solved the problem of dealing in an interesting way with the historical information that has to be conveyed, and at the same time getting a sense of reality about the daily life of the characters" (Strick and Houston 138). Not even his beloved Ophuls could pass muster, as Kubrick expressed disappointment in *Lola Montes* (Haine 309).

(In later years, Kubrick admired, as mentioned above, Wajda's *Danton*, with his assistant Anthony Frewin later reporting that Kubrick had considered it "perhaps the finest historical film ever made" [Wrigley]. *Danton* stars Gerard Depardieu as the titular architect of the Reign of Terror who finds himself a victim of it, famously saying that "The Revolution eats its children." One wonders if there wasn't some degree of self-congratulation in Kubrick's admiration for the film, as its musical score by Jean Prodromidès is highly reminiscent of the vocal pieces of Ligeti used to accompany The Monolith in *2001*, where the shifting, uneasy atonalities create a sense of dread; this turns certain of *Danton*'s scenes into those more suited to a horror film – it was the Reign of *Terror*, after all.)

Like *Barry Lyndon*, *Gone with the Wind* features a late sequence in which the young child of the film's central couple dies after being thrown from a horse. The sequence of Bonnie's death in *Wind* is very short, with the foreshadowing laid on heavily as the scene progresses. The death drives conflict between Rhett and Scarlett, though on its heels the ailment and death of another character dilutes its impact. *Barry Lyndon*, of course, eschews foreshadowing in this case in favor of early revelation; another virtue Kubrick detected in the voiceover was that it provides "hints in advance of the most important plot developments, thus lessening the risk of their seeming contrived" (Ciment 170). This thirst for authenticity, visible in the locations, costumes, lighting (Ciment: "Why do you prefer natural lighting?" Kubrick: "Because it's the way we see things" [176]), and other visual detail, seems part of a design to assure the film rests in "tragedy" that "can assimilate the twists and turns of the plot without becoming melodrama," according to the director. "Melodrama uses all the problems of the world, and the difficulties and disasters with befall the characters, to demonstrate that the world is, after all, a benevolent and just place" (173-174).

"The questions are always, is it true? Is it interesting?" Kubrick told Tim Cahill (Cahill 374). For Kubrick, "true" and "interesting" precluded melodrama as he defined it. In the context of *Barry Lyndon*, Ciment wrote that "for Kubrick the eighteenth century is rotten to the core, an age awaiting its impending destruction; behind the facade of gaiety, luxury and pleasure, death and disintegration are already lurking" (Ciment 66). But this worldview was not limited to the eighteenth century; *Dr. Strangelove* is explicitly the tale of the *twentieth* century "awaiting [or causing] its impending destruction." So his opposition to *Gone with the Wind* likely started with its idealistic opening scroll:

> There was a land of Cavaliers and Cotton Fields called the Old South …
> Here in the pretty world Gallantry took its last bow..
> Here was the last ever to be seen of Knights and their Ladies Fair, of Master and of Slave …
> Look for it only in books, for it is no more than a dream remembered.
> A Civilization gone with the wind.

Kubrick's response might well have been "good riddance," but he found in in the pages of Thackeray the words that more pithily (though in reference to a different age) lay waste to the notion of romanticizing a civilization "rotten to the core:"

It was in the reign of King George III
That the aforesaid personages lived and quarreled;
Good or bad, handsome or ugly, rich or poor
They are all equal now

Petty quests for status, for peerage, for paintings by Ludovico Cardi, are all equalized in death. *Barry Lyndon* stands not only as a corrective to the idealizations of *Gone with the Wind*, but to any attempt at a historical film that declines to present the truth of historical reality – and contemporary reality, for that matter.

Whereas the structure of *Gone with the Wind* allows Rhett and Scarlett little time to mourn their fallen daughter before the next misfortune befalls them, *Barry Lyndon* gives substantial weight to the effect of Bryan's tragic death upon the inner and outer lives of Barry and Lady Lyndon. Barry turns to drink, burying himself in the bottle to such an extent that his mother must order the estate's servants to carry him to bed. Lady Lyndon finds her comfort in religion, praying fervently alongside the Reverend Runt, what makeup she dons smeared with tears that turn her eyes red, her face its palest shade. The sarabande, back to its gentler arrangement, continues over these sad vignettes.

The power vacuum at the head of the household is filled by Barry's mother. Once a "rustic", she is now authoritative and commanding, reviewing the many bills with Graham. It is she who calls in the Reverend Runt to fire him, accusing him of being the cause of Lady Lyndon's fragile emotional state, and waving off his (correct) assessment that she and her son have brought to near-ruin "a fine family fortune." In the causal structure of the film, this leads to Lady Lyndon's suicide attempt, her suffering therefrom shot with a handheld camera. The Narrator practically gloats when he reports that this attempt brings "overdue" intervention from Lord Bullingdon.

While some have famously offered that tracking shots have sufficient intrinsic meaning so as to be "a matter of morality," discovering a consistent attitude in tracking shots across Kubrick's films is no easy task. Robert Kolker rightly points out that in his films "we learn more about a character from the way that character inhabits a particular space than [...] from what a character says" (Kolker 101), and attempts to find consistent meaning in the director's use of camera movement. Kubrick is "inclined to use the moving camera as a surrogate or parallel for the point of view of a character" (103), he observes, using as his primary example the tracking shot preceding Alex and he browses through a record boutique in *A*

Clockwork Orange. While allowing that his analysis is oversimplified, Kolker notes that the camera movement in concert with Alex's posture, behavior, and the color and music (Wendy Carlos' electronified arrangement of the "Turkish March" passage of "Lovely Lovely Ludwig Van" Beethoven's "Glorious Ninth") "indicate[s] total control" (ibid.). He also points to contrasting tracking shots in *Paths of Glory*, which at one point dramatize the "control" Kirk Douglas' Colonel Dax has as he struts through he trenches, contrasted with the lack of control the condemned soldiers have as tracking shots lead them to their execution (105). But another interesting point of comparison for the Alex record store shot is that of the tracking shot that accompanies Lord Bullingdon into the gentleman's club where he demands satisfaction from Barry. The shots resemble each other in surface ways, not the least of which is the fact that Alex's dandyish costume is reprised in Bullingdon's outfit; both shots also aren't linear, as Alex walks in a circle and Bullingdon must take a winding route through the club to find Barry. But Alex is indeed in control, confident to the point of arrogance, showing off in front of the store workers as he makes his way to two young girls he intends to seduce. Bullingdon has purpose, but he lacks confidence; his anxiety is palpable in his timid movements, facial expressions, and the tone of his voice once he addresses Barry – the overwhelming majority of the plot and character information we draw from this scene comes from nonverbal cues – "the way that character inhabits a particular space." But, as also alluded to by Kolker as quoted above, the setting and sound also create this impact: whereas the record store is bright and colorful and the music jaunty, the lighting here is dark, the décor drab, with attendants napping in their chairs and a maid scrubbing the floor, while the music marks a return of the duel arrangement of the sarabande that was previously heard when Barry "vanquished" Quin.

In Kent Jones' documentary *Hitchcock/Truffaut*, David Fincher says that part of a director's job is taking "things that should be really fast and making them slow, and [taking] things that should be really slow and making them fast." We have seen how Kubrick uses three-shot series to convey passages of time, and at one point even uses a direct cut to move the story eight years. But the climactic duel with Bullingdon is an occasion to slow things down. Whereas the Barry-Quin duel is disposed of fairly quickly, the Barry-Bullingdon one is presented in nine minutes of nearly real-time depiction (there may be a quick elision of time when the second set of guns is loaded). In fact, this climactic duel is in many ways the direct opposite of the initial one. Whereas Barry was once the upstart challenging an older man to fight over a lover, here Bullingdon takes Barry's place to fight over a mother. Bullingdon takes Barry's place physically, as well, aiming from left-to-right, the position occupied by Barry prior. The Quin duel opens with a shot of a pistol being loaded, which then zooms out to reveal the opponents dwarfed by the landscape; here a similar shot opens the scene, but instead of a zoom we simply cut to another angle. There is no imposing (yet beautiful) landscape here, as the combatants find themselves in an enclosed space – the world is closing in on Barry Lyndon.

Bullingdon is shot at medium length from a low angle, as if to represent his societal advantage as a lord; Barry is shot with a long lens in close-up, the world blurred behind him, as he stands alone in this time of trial. Yet the two duels echo in one important way: in both confrontations, Barry is the calmer man. Bullingdon's fidgety uncertainty causes him to discharge his gun prematurely, his bullet flying harmlessly into the ground. Much to his amazement and disappointment, this "counts" as his shot, and he must stand his ground as Barry has the opportunity to fire upon him; his fearful vomiting is looked upon shamefully by the nobles in attendance.

What happens now is one of cinema's most enduring yet underdiscussed mysteries: why does Barry fire into the ground, thus sparing the life of a man known to harbor extreme ill will for him? Kolker says that here Barry, "as always, tries to bring some humanity to" the situation by firing into the ground (161), raising the question as to which cut of the film he saw. Barry is a carrier of humanity? "But, as in every other instance when Barry tries to humanize the world," he continues, "he suffers for it" (ibid.). Yet the "humanity" we typically see from Barry is his human *folly*, his inability to control his passions, his resistance to societal strictures. Sparing Bullingdon has little commonality with his throwing a glass in Quin's face, his delaying sojourn with Lischen, his committing adultery where his wife can easily find him, or his physical assault on Bullingdon at the recital. The only other acts of mercy or tenderness we see from Barry are in relation to his blood, his mother and son. This choice during the duel *breaks* the pattern of his behavior – it is his "crisis of existential significance."

So what does his choice existentially signify? The Narrator, who has been all too eager to give an accounting of Barry's baser instincts, granting him a positive appraisal only in regards to his love for Bryan, remains absolutely silent throughout the sequence, easily his lengthiest pause. And as this sequence is entirely invented by Kubrick (Barry's final fall in the novel is engineered by a former lover of Lady Lyndon's, and what vengeance Bullingdon visits upon Barry is recounted entirely in one line in the "editor's" addendum: "[Lord Bullingdon] revenged upon [Barry's] person the insults of former days" [Thackeray]), we don't even have the novel to reference. Clearly, the filmmaker is challenging us to come to our own conclusions as to Barry's motivations. Penelope Houston finds the act consistent not with Barry's "humanity" but with his "devious career" that "has been governed by the ambition to become a gentleman; and it's as a 'gentleman' that he holds off when he has his man at his mercy [...] Bullingdon, who has the advantage of having been born a gentleman, shows no such compunction" (Houston). James Naremore similarly, but less sinisterly, finds Barry's choice an act of "gallantry" (Naremore 182). Thomas Allen Nelson believes the moment is intended "to indicate Barry's capacity to act independent of a fortuitous turn of chance," and is "one instance in the film where the elaborate mechanics of social form embody a correspondingly significant moral and emotional content" (Nelson 192-193). Gene Phillips and Rodney Hill find it a sign that "the last spark of real warmth and human love" in Barry was not "extinguished" by his son's death (Phillips and Hill 272).

Can all of these observers, and the many others not cited here, be simultaneously correct? Their explanations are compatible, and in fact complementary: Barry, demonstrating his humanity and attempting to fit into gentlemanly society, ironically finds that the gentlemanly thing is actually the *right* thing – and that he is punished for not only doing the right thing but also for his societal pretension.

There is another possibility I would like to offer: perhaps it is not merely mercy for the younger version of himself Barry might see in Bullingdon, nor merely is it a gentlemanly demurral that only the societally disadvantaged need make, but this may be an act of kindness toward *Lady Lyndon*, as well. She has been traumatized by the death of her younger son, and, lacking the spiritual guidance of her chaplain, has made an attempt on her own life. Could Barry be reluctant to cast upon his wife the loss of yet another child? We have not seen, at any point, any sincere affection directed from Barry to his wife; we know his seduction of her to have been motivated by pursuit of her fortune, with no "romantic notions" involved. We may be generous and find his apology over kissing the maid as the act of a repentant heart, but, if so, why does Barry wait an entire evening before seeking forgiveness the next morning? Bryan begged on his death bed that Barry and Lady Lyndon act kindly to each other, so that they all might meet again; is it possible that Barry has taken this admonishment to heart, and thus refuses to take action that, while it might save him, would harm her?

Whatever Barry's motivations, Bullingdon lacks them. "I have not received ... satisfaction," stammers the large-lipped lord (#mickjaggerfirstdrafts), and, for the first time, we see a glint of fear in Barry's eyes. In every encounter of his life, Barry has been the man of lower status, but he has never shown fear. But now he stands hopeless, isolated in telephoto close-up (similar to the close-ups used on Colonel Dax as he helplessly watches the execution of his men, and a relatively long-lens medium shot of Dr. Harford as he attempts to comprehend Victor Ziegler's account of his foiled erotic misadventures and investigation, in all cases the world out of focus around protagonists defeated). Bullingdon's shot makes an impact, and Barry cries out in agony.

This act of violence has made a man of Lord Bullingdon; he is assertive in giving commands to the household servants, drawing from Reverend Runt what Kubrick classified a "little smile of triumph" which "tells you all you need to know regarding the way he feels about Barry's misfortune," given that he "is secretly in love with Lady Lyndon in his own prim, repressed little way" (Ciment 171). And Barry is metaphorically castrated, losing his left leg beneath the knee (Barry argues with his surgeon about this, but it is in a later zoom-out from a sedate Barry that we learn that the leg has in fact been amputated).

For the second straight film, a Kubrick protagonist finds his story at an end in a surgical bed. The film becomes more subjective here, for the first time utilizing a direct shot from Barry's point of view. He plays his chaste game of cards with his mother, the bookend to the racy game played with Nora once upon a time. When Graham comes to deliver the terms by which Barry is being asked to leave the country (the first substantial lines Philip Stone gets to deliver, after having been present for much of the film's second half), Barry and his mother accept reality with equanimity. As always, narrational content about Barry is given by another character as we see a close-up of Barry, in this instance when Graham outlines his debts and the likely consequences ("jail") thereof.

The sarabande had been playing for much of this, fading out upon Graham's entrance. The Schubert Trio makes its unlikely return along with a cut to an establishing shot of the inn where Barry recuperates. Barry exits on crutches, making his way to the carriage that will apparently begin his journey from England. The Narrator, at last, admits his own limitations, stating that, though Barry took up his "former profession of a gambler, without his former success," "we have not the means of following accurately" the balance of his life in any detail. Barry drops his crutches behind him, his mother reaching out for them, as the shot freeze-frames. The camera is behind Barry, as are his hopes and aspirations; he disappears from us, once and forever, defeated and crippled, frozen in agony and time: Antoine Doinel in reverse.

It seems that this is where the film should end, but Kubrick has a habit of ending films in unexpected places (or perhaps *you* knew that the apes of

2001's Dawn of Man would result in a giant baby floating in space?). "He never saw Lady Lyndon again," The Narrator says over the freeze-frame (his last line), but the same is not true of the audience. We cut to a Castle Hackton interior. Lord Bullingdon, in greyed wig and pale makeup, hands Lady Lyndon checks to sign, Graham and Runt in attendance. Lady Lyndon looks more ghostly than ever, hollow and ashen. Yet she signs the checks without reaction.

Until comes the one to Barry Lyndon; this is his yearly annuity, his bounty for staying away. She pauses; she looks into space. The deep trills of the Trio belie a rumbling. Though Barry is not in this scene (one of the rare scenes in this film to which this applies), his presence is inescapable. Where Barry struggled to make his impact in a society unwelcoming to his insurgence, we see here that he has made an unforgettable and negative impact on Lady Lyndon. We do not see Barry, but we see his consequence.

Bullingdon looks on as his mother returns to her check. The date is December of 1789, roughly five months into the societal upheaval in France that led to its own consequences across the continent and the world. Is British society doomed as well? It is impossible for these characters to know – what doom concerns the denizens of this room is the domestic doom of the Lyndon estate. We might note that this is the room with the large family portrait, which we last saw dwarfing Barry and Bryan, the weight of its mighty expectations overwhelming the (for now) living beings below, those whose pettiness and vanity and social striving will all be turned to dust and rendered "equal" by the "grim invincible enemy" that stalks them (us) all. Where once this room hosted a happy scene, it now is a site of sadness and regret, of tragedy, and in the shadow of the painting on the wall, Kubrick's final painterly composition might carry a title of its own: *The Doom of Barry Lyndon.*

In conversation with Peter Labuza, film critic and *Barry Lyndon* enthusiast Bilge Ebiri noted that making an epic of the life of Barry Lyndon is more daring than an epic biography of Napoleon would have been (Labuza); after all, significant, epoch-defining historical figures are routinely subject to such treatment, but Barry is ultimately a footnote even in the fictional world that contains him. There is something oddly perverse about devoting so much screentime to a figure of so little import, and whose adventures and misadventures, while compelling, are not strikingly unique. Yet it is in this everyday nature of his troubles that viewers from the isolated English countryside to metropolitan New York to the urban/suburban sprawl of Los Angeles, be they born 1928 or 1978 or, I, daresay, 2028, see themselves. For the strategy of focusing on small details as a gateway into an understanding of a larger world is embedded into the film's design, as we have seen with the prevalent zoom-out scene-setting strategy, and as we see again in the Lyndon family's domestic aspirations and troubles finding rhymes not only in the past (paintings on the walls), but in the future (as revolution rages a channel away). The specific becomes the general, and one man's vanities and misfortunes become his society's and, in turn, our own; while the costumes and underlying mores may shift over time, in the end, Barry's and his contemporaries' psychological, sexual, political, and personal conflicts are equalized with ours: *Barry Lyndon* is "a film about the basic questions of our own times," and of *all* times.

Can any movie be bigger than that?

BIBLIOGRAPHY

Alcott, John. Interviewed in "Photographing Stanley Kubrick's *Barry Lyndon* – John Alcott" from *American Cinematographer*, December, 1975, accessed at http://www.visualmemory.co.uk/sk/2001a/bl/page1.htm.

Aldiss, Brian. "Meet the Man Behind the Myth" from *The Observer*, March 14, 1999, accessed at http://www.visual-memory.co.uk/sk/memories/page5.htm.

Aumont, Jacques, translated by Timothy Barnard. *Montage – Second Edition, Revised and Expanded* (Caboose, 2014).

Bogdanovich, Peter. "What They Say about Stanley Kubrick" from *The New York Times Magazine*, July 4, 1999, accessed at http://www.nytimes.com/1999/07/04/magazine/what-they-say-about-stanley-kubrick.html.

Bordwell, David. *Narration in the Fiction Film* (The University of Wisconsin Press, 1985).

Cahill, Tim. "Stanley Kubrick" from *Rolling Stone*, August 27, 1987 in *The Rolling Stone Film Reader*, ed. Peter Travers (Pocket Books, 1996).

Castle, Alison, ed. *The Stanley Kubrick Archives* (Taschen, 2005).

Castle, Alison, ed. "Notes" in *Stanley Kubrick's "Napoleon": The Greatest Movie Never Made* (Taschen, 2011).

Charlie Rose. Interview with Christiane Kubrick, Jan Harlan, and Martin Scorsese. Accessed at https://www.youtube.com/watch?v=VrtJXH2hRGI.

Ciment, Michel. *Kubrick: The Definitive Edition* (Faber and Faber, Inc., 2001).

Cocks, Geoffrey. *The Wolf at the Door: Stanley Kubrick, History, & the Holocaust* (Peter Lang Publishing, Inc., 2004).

Crowe, Cameron. *Conversations with Wilder* (Alfred A. Knopft, 1999).

66

DiGiulio, Ed. "Two Special Lenses for *Barry Lyndon*" from *American Cinematographer*, December, 1975, accessed at http://www.visual-memory.co.uk/sk/ac/len/page1.htm.

Ellis, Geoffrey, annotator. "Stanley Kubrick/Felix Markham Napoleon Dialogues" in *Stanley Kubrick's "Napoleon": The Greatest Movie Never Made*, ed. Alison Castle (Taschen, 2011).

Fischer, Ralf Michael. "Pictures at an Exhibition? Allusions and Illusions in *Barry Lyndon*" in *Stanley Kubrick – Second, revised edition* (Deutsches Filmmuseum, 2007).

Foix, Vicente Molina. "An interview with Stanley Kubrick" from *El Pais Artes*, December 20, 1980, in *The Stanley Kubrick Archives*, ed. Alison Castle (Taschen, 2005).

Frayling, Christopher. *Sergio Leone: Something to Do with Death* (Faber and Faber Limited, 2000).

Frewin, Anthony. "Stanley Kubrick: Writers, Writing, Reading" in *The Stanley Kubrick Archives*, ed. Alison Castle (Taschen, 2005).

Gelmis, Joseph. *The Film Director as Superstar* (Doubleday & Company, Inc., 1970).

Gengaro, Christine Lee. *Listening to Stanley Kubrick: The Music in His Films* (Rowman & Littlefield, 2012).

Godard, Jean-Luc. "Stanley Kubrick" from "Dictionary of American Filmmakers" in *Cahiers du Cinema*, 150-151, translated by Tom Milne in *Godard on Godard* (The Viking Press, Inc., 1972).

Haine, Raymond. "Good Morning Mr. Kubrick" in *Cahiers du Cinema*, July 1957, in *The Stanley Kubrick Archives*, ed. Alison Castle (Taschen, 2005).

Herr, Michael. Forward to *Full Metal Jacket* screenplay. 1987, accessed at http://www.visual-memory.co.uk/amk/doc/0079.html.

Herr, Michael. "Kubrick" from *Vanity Fair*, April 2000, accessed at http://www.vanityfair.com/hollywood/2010/04/kubrick-199908.

Hitchcock/Truffaut. Directed by Kent Jones, written by Kent Jones & Serge

Toubiana. Released by Cohen Media Group.

Houston, Penelope. *"Barry Lyndon"* from *Sight & Sound*, Spring, 1976, accessed at http://www.visual-memory.co.uk/sk/ss/barrylyndon.htm.

James, Nick. "At home with the Kubricks" from *Sight & Sound*, September 1999.

Kael, Pauline. "Kubrick's Guilded Age" from *The New Yorker*, December 29, 1975.

Kagan, Norman. *The Cinema of Stanley Kubrick: New Expanded Edition* (The Continuum Publishing Company, 1995).

Klein, Michael. "Narrative and Discourse in Kubrick's Modern Tragedy" in *The English Novel and the Movies*, ed. Michael Klein and Gillian Parker (Frederick Ungar Publishing Co., 1982), accessed at http://www.visual-memory.co.uk/amk/doc/0028.html.

Kolker, Robert. *A Cinema of Loneliness: Penn, Stone, Kubrick, Scorsese, – Third Edition* (Oxford University Press, 2000).

Kubrick, Stanley. "Kubrick's 'Notes on Film'" from *The Observer Weekend Review*, December 4, 1960, accessed at http://www.visual-memory.co.uk/amk/doc/0076.html.

Kubrick, Stanley. *Napoleon: A Screenplay*, draft dated September 29, 1969, in *Stanley Kubrick's "Napoleon": The Greatest Movie Never Made*, ed. Alison Castle (Taschen, 2011).

Kubrick, Stanley. Letter to the Editor of the *New York Times*, February 27, 1972, in *The Stanley Kubrick Archives*, ed. Alison Castle (Taschen, 2005).

Labuza, Peter. *The Cinephiliacs #5 – Bilge Ebiri (*Barry Lyndon*)*, podcast published September 10, 2012, accessed at http://www.thecinephiliacs.net/2012/09/episode-5-bilge-ebiri-barry-lyndon.html.

LoBrutto, Vincent. *Stanley Kubrick: A Biography* (Penguin Group, 1997).
Ljujić, Tatjana. "Painterly Immediacy in Kubrick's *Barry Lyndon*" in *Stanley Kubrick: New Perspectives*, ed. Tatjana Ljujić, Peter Kramer, and Richard Daniels (Black Dog Publishing, 2015).

68

McAvoy, Catriona. "Interview with Diane Johnson" in *The Shining: Studies in the Horror Film*, ed. Daniel Olson (Centipede Press, 2015).

Mikics, David. *Stanley Kubrick: American Filmmaker* (Yale University Press, 2020).

Naremore, James. *On Kubrick* (British Film Institute, 2007).

Nelson, Thomas Allen. *Kubrick: A Film Artist's Maze – New and Expanded Edition* (Indiana University Press, 2000).

Nordern, Eric. "Playboy Interview: Stanley Kubrick" from *Playboy*, September 1968, in *The Making of Kubrick's 2001*, ed. Jerome Agel (Signet, 1970).

Nicolson, Adam. "World on the verge of collapse", accessed at http://www.tate.org.uk/context-comment/articles/world-on-verge-collapse

Phillips, Gene D. & Rodney Hill. *The Encyclopedia of Stanley Kubrick* (Checkmark Books, 2002).

Pizzello, Stephen. "A Sword in the Bed" from *American Cinematographer*, October, 1999, accessed at https://www.theasc.com/magazine/oct99/sword/pg1.htm.

Pulver, Andrew. "Stanley Kubrick: the *Barry Lyndon* archives – in pictures" from *The Guardian* Online, December 10, 2015, accessed at https://www.theguardian.com/film/gallery/2015/dec/10/stanley-kubrick-the-barry-lyndon-archives-in-pictures.

Raphael, Frederic. *Eyes Wide Open: A Memoir of Stanley Kubrick* (Ballantine Books, 1999).

Schaefer, Dennis and Larry Salvato. *Masters of Light: Conversations with Contemporary Cinematographers* (University of California Press, 1984).

Schickel, Richard. "Kubrick's Grandest Gamble" from *Time*, December 15, 1975, in *Stanley Kubrick: Interviews*, ed. Gene D. Phillips (University Press of Mississippi, 2001).

Six Kinds of Light: John Alcott. Accessed at https://www.youtube.com/watch?v=_E8C-3MU00g.

Strick, Philip and Penelope Houston. "Modern Times: An Interview with Stanley Kubrick" from *Sight & Sound*, Spring, 1972, in *Stanley Kubrick: Interviews*, ed. Gene D. Phillips (University Press of Mississippi, 2001).

Thackeray, William Makepeace. *The Memoirs of Barry Lyndon, Esq.* (Project Gutenberg eBook published at http://www.gutenberg.org/files/4558/4558-h/4558-h.htm).

Thackeray, William Makepeace. *Vanity Fair.* (Project Gutenberg eBook published at http://www.gutenberg.org/files/599/599-h/599-h.htm).

Thompson, Richard. Paul Schrader/Richard Thompson interview in *Film Comment*, March/April 1976, accessed at http://www.filmcomment.com/article/paul-schrader-richard-thompson-interview/.

Walker, Alexander and Sybil Taylor and Ulrich Ruchti. *Stanley Kubrick, Director: A Visual Analysis* (W.W. Norton & Company, 1999).

Wickre, Bill. "Pictures, Plurality, and Puns: A Visual Approach to *Barry Lyndon*" in *Depth of Field: Stanley Kubrick, Film, and the Uses of History*, ed. Geoffrey Cocks, James Diedrick, and Glenn Perusek (The University of Wisconsin Press, 2006).

Wrigley, Nick. "Stanley Kubrick, cinephile" from *Sight & Sound* Online, updated July 25, 2016, accessed at http://www.bfi.org.uk/news-opinion/sight-sound-magazine/polls-surveys/stanley-kubrick-cinephile.

Young, Colin. "The Hollywood War of Independence" from *Film Quarterly*, Spring 1959, in *Stanley Kubrick: Interviews*, ed. Gene D. Phillips (University Press of Mississippi, 2001).

INDEX

Made in the USA
Las Vegas, NV
28 January 2024